VOICES OF HOPE:

The Story of the Jane Addams School for Democracy

Edited by: Nan Kari and Nan Skelton

Voices of Hope: The Story of the Jane Addams School for Democracy is published by Kettering Foundation Press. The interpretations and conclusions contained in this book represent the views of the authors. They do not necessarily reflect the views of the Charles F. Kettering Foundation, its trustees, or its officers.

For information about permission to reproduce selections from this book, write to:

> Permissions
> Kettering Foundation Press
> 200 Commons Road
> Dayton, Ohio 45459

This book is printed on acid-free paper.
First edition 2007
Manufactured in the United States of America

ISBN-978-0-923993-19-1

Library of Congress Control Number: 2006934687

All of the photographs that appear in this book were taken by staff members or volunteer participants of the Jane Addams School for Democracy to be used for materials and publications related to the school. Permission to use them in *Voices of Hope* was granted to the Kettering Foundation Press by the school's codirectors, Nan Skelton and Nan Kari.

ACKNOWLEDGMENTS

We wish to acknowledge the creative spirit and continued support of John Wallace and Sandy Fuller, the other cofounders of the Jane Addams School. Peter Leach has been the "unofficial" JAS photographer for ten years, sharing his talents with great humor. Many of the photos in this edition are attributed to him. Ilse Tebbetts, our editor, shared our enthusiasm, saw new angles, and helped us envision and bring to fruition an integrated whole. Thanks also to Harry Boyte and Nick Longo who read early drafts and offered encouragement. We are especially appreciative of the staff at the Center for Democracy and Citizenship, who believe wholeheartedly in the democratic vision that propels and sustains this work. Finally, without the generous support from the Kettering Foundation, the Bush Foundation, the Otto Bremer Foundation, and the Freeman Foundation, the Jane Addams School for Democracy would not have had this story to tell.

For John and David Skelton

For Jonathan and Ana Kari

CONTENTS

FOREWORD

A couple of years ago, I was asked by a local organization to reflect on what it means to be an American.

"To be an American," I wrote, "is to believe that I CAN. I can become anybody. I can do anything. I hold the power to direct my own opportunities and influence my own circumstances."

This is the story of the Jane Addams School for Democracy. As Voices of Hope will show, this democracy cannot be manufactured or purchased. It evolves only from the lives of those who believe in it, live it, and feed its perpetuation for today and for future generations. Read it, live it, and let its inspiration liberate all of us to be better Americans.

The inspiring stories told in this book could be my story as well.

Twenty-five years ago, my family came to this country with nothing but a couple of backpacks. Yet we never felt poor or disadvantaged. My parents saw every job as a new opportunity for a brand new beginning to a better future. They lived everyday as a second chance to watch their children grow up with hope and optimism. Even when they had to pick pickles, clean toilets, mop floors, and chop onions on an assembly line to provide my brothers and sisters and me with a clean home, hot lunches, and school supplies, they were hopeful. They believed that an America that was willing to help people like them was an America that could do more for their children. My siblings and I have reaped abundantly from their sacrifices and their wisdom.

Every day, I look at my mother and my father, and I am in awe of the terrifying journey they undertook on foot, by rowboat, by bus, and across the ocean on a flying "metal eagle" to find haven in this country. I am humbled by the fears, uncertainties, and doubts they had to overcome and the courage they had to muster from deep, deep down—*the resolve it must have taken to live one day at a time until they felt safe and secure and welcome to call this country home.*

When I was elected to the legislature in January 2002, a reporter asked my father how he felt about having his daughter elected to the Minnesota State Senate. My father replied, "I am very happy. My daughter, my senator, my country. I belong."

To be an American is to be infused by a spirit and a hope that must be deeply cherished, but generously shared. It is a spirit that is renewed by every generation of new Americans. It is a spirit that allowed a little refugee girl from the mountains of Laos, the opportunity to become a Minnesota state senator. I have my parents to thank for this. And thanks are due also to the many generations of he-roes and she-roes who sacrificed to make this country what it is today. In their honor, and in the name of the millions around the world who continue to live in silence and oppression, we must not shy away from our responsibilities as citizens and as activists.

Both staff and students, both children and adults at the Jane Addams School are clear about these responsibilities. There is nothing traditional about this school except perhaps its passionate dedication to the principles that have made this nation strong: embracing differences, contributing to a larger purpose, and practicing democracy. All its participants are teachers and learners. And all of them come to understand that each of them not only CAN, but must, if we are to preserve our legacy: a government of, for, and by the people.

The vision of the Founding Fathers was that the colonists could "form a more perfect union." Work at the Jane Addams School is dedicated to forming "more perfect communities." And who is to say that we may not one day achieve one or both of these goals?

Senator Mee Moua
Minnesota State Senate
August 2006

PREFACE

We grew up in a time not long after the Holocaust and the United States internment of Japanese Americans had occurred. Several decades passed before the voices of protest began to emerge. The silence was haunting. Where were those who knew and refused to speak? Why did it take so long to develop a collective voice? What causes a democratic people to lose voice? These questions and the realization that people chose not to speak left deep impressions.

The crucible of this history fired our passion to change structures and practices in higher education, in public schools, and in neighborhoods, with the hope that a legacy of change will contribute to a flourishing democracy. We are now convinced that a living democracy requires the contributions and responsible actions of all people. Finding multiple ways for people to take action can have immense impact on our society's contemporary civic malaise.

A MESSAGE FROM THE PRESIDENT OF THE UNITED STATES

We have tackled questions of how to affect individual and collective change for nearly four decades in multiple roles—as mothers, teachers, community organizers, and members of committees and task forces at the local, state, and national levels. Our paths, though different, converged around the core belief that

a small group of people can lay the foundation for a different kind of house—a structure built brick by brick, with many hands, to seed people's passion for re-vitalizing our democracy. We've gathered builders with good spirit, wisdom, and many diverse talents and experiences to help construct the Jane Addams School for Democracy. In ten years, we have laid a solid foundation.

Our intent in writing this book is to invite the reader to join us in reviving our democracy. We have seen that democratic possibility exists wherever imagination and creativity are unleashed. We show through the stories gathered in these pages that democracy will survive if we do not let our voices grow silent.

Why does the story need to be told now? The Jane Addams School for Democracy is a concrete, practical, on-the-ground democratic effort that works. It is also an intellectual project, through which we believe important lessons can be gleaned for the broader society. Because the Jane Addams School calls people to go beyond building community within an immediate location, it opens a pathway into the public world, where people find themselves able to address deep injustices. It is in this context that people experience a collective sense of transformative power.

Our primary approach in writing this book is to go beyond scholarly texts and well-recognized research, to draw in the voices of those who have often been written about but have seldom told their own stories. Thus we have collected essays from participants as well as interviews and photographs of those whose work has created the Jane Addams School for Democracy.

—*Nan Skelton and Nan Kari*

Nan Skelton (left) and Nan Kari

Part One:
THEN AND NOW

DEMOCRACY FROM THE GROUND UP

by Nan Kari and Nan Skelton

The roots of the Jane Addams School for Democracy grew from the life experiences, values, and public passions of those who came together in 1996 with a vision to create a democratic organization and egalitarian way of working and learning across cultures. The democratic traditions of progressive twentieth-century leaders like Jane Addams, Ella Baker, Myles Horton, and John Dewey inspire our work. From the beginning, we intended that JAS would address large questions about education and democracy.

We claim authority to engage in such work from an understanding of democracy as a living philosophy, an unfinished work to be taken up by every generation of people who claim power and identity as active citizens.

A passion for serious educational reform animated early conversations and writing by students and other founders. An early analysis found in the JAS archival papers, describes the contemporary education crisis in this way:

Students' own lives, cultures, and backgrounds are rarely seen as learning resources. . . . Educational institutions are disconnected from the places in which they are located. Conversely, surrounding communities are rarely seen as rich with cultures and settings that provide opportunities for learning. . . . There are few opportunities for students to reflect deeply on the moral implications of what they are learning. . . . There is an unmet need in our educational system to engage young people in work of public importance.[1]

We started with the assumption that U.S.-born young people together with immigrant families could cultivate civic identities and learn democratic skills through involvement in serious public work. Building the Jane Addams School was and continues to be a public work to which many have contributed. It has provided us the context to better understand concepts and practices of democratic education.

Guiding Traditions

The writings of Jane Addams, particularly her descriptions of Hull House, the philosophy and popular-education pedagogy developed at the Highlander Folk School and later, the practices used by the citizenship schools that helped catalyze the civil rights movement of the 1950s and 1960s, informed our thinking as we launched JAS.

In some ways, JAS is a reincarnation of the late-nineteenth- and early-twentieth-century settlement house. Canon Barnett, who founded the first settlement in East London, called Toynbee Hall, described the distinguishing feature as "the absence of program and the presence of men and women who recognize the obligations of citizenship."[2] Addams and her colleague, Ellen Gates Starr recognized the radical power shift embedded in this model, which greatly influenced her founding of one of the first U.S. settlements in Chicago. Located in an immigrant neighborhood on Chicago's West Side, the people of Hull House addressed a variety of social problems, as immigrants also educated themselves through classes in English and a range of

topics. The Hull House connection with faculty and students from the University of Chicago formed a reciprocal institutional relationship and helped define one of the key elements of the settlement model. Likewise, students and faculty from the

University of Minnesota and local colleges join with immigrant participants at JAS to connect academic learning to issues of place and public life.

Addams held clear ideas about the roles of professional educators and the talents of ordinary people.

She believed that everyone deserved educational opportunities and that people could learn to be bold, confident, public-spirited actors with skills for self-governance and capacities to cocreate a robust common world through their labor. In fact, she believed a democratic society depended on it. In her essay "Educational Methods," she writes of the teacher's role:

> We are gradually requiring of the educator that he shall free the powers of each man and connect him with the rest of life. We ask this not merely because it is the man's right to be thus connected, but because we have become convinced that the social order cannot afford to get along without his special contribution.[3]

This same conviction—that immigrants can and do make civic contributions, whether or not they hold legal citizenship status—is centrally embedded in the philosophy and mission of JAS.

In 1932, in rural, eastern Tennessee, Myles Horton founded the Highlander Folk School, a powerful catalyst for social change during the early labor union and civil rights movements. In 1930, Horton attended the University of Chicago and

became acquainted with John Dewey, Jane Addams, and other leaders in the settlement movement. Although they shared similar democratic values and goals in promoting adult education, Horton felt settlements had moved away from the founding vision to become constrained by organizational structures. He believed people have the capacity to educate and govern themselves but need the opportunity to practice it. He wanted Highlander staff to encourage participants to make decisions and help run the school. Horton found greater resonance with the Danish folk-school model in which students and teachers lived together, with ample opportunity for peer learning. Principles of peer learning informed the richly textured pedagogy at Highlander that grounds people in their experiences and passion for social justice as it draws on music, art, dance, storytelling, and cultural knowledge as resources for social change. By 1944, in defiance of the law, Highlander became an important gathering place for blacks and whites to study together. Ten years later, in anticipation of the Supreme Court's ruling on desegregation, Highlander received a grant to help lay the groundwork

for citizenship schools, a popular-education approach to help blacks prepare for citizenship.[4]

The idea of nonprofessional learning partnerships, a practice embraced by JAS, was embedded in the approach used in the citizenship schools that sprung up during the civil rights movement in the 1960s. These schools avoided using certified teachers because, according to Bernice Robinson, one of the first teachers, "People with teaching experience would likely impose their schooling methodology on the students and be judgmental." The first time people got together, Robinson would say to them, "I am not a teacher. We're here to learn together. You're going to teach me as much as I'm going to teach you." She began where learners were and incorporated their interests into the informal curriculum that learners helped to construct:

> I talked with each one individually. . . . Some could read a little, and some could sign their names. I asked them what they wanted to learn. The responses included: to make out a catalogue order blank, to read the Bible, to read letters from grown-up children living

away from home, to write their name in cursive.[5] At the founding of JAS, we imagined a similar process of informal, self-directed learning might also resonate with new immigrants, many of whom have no formal schooling. There were no blueprints. We determined to figure this out together.

The traditions of democratic education developed through the settlement movement and in the popular-education movement that took root at places like Highlander Folk School and in the citizenship schools, helped us begin to identify the values that would guide the work of the first year: Everyone has the capacity to teach and to learn; cultures and lived experience hold rich learning resources; ordinary people can affect social change. Although we would come to understand much more deeply what these values meant and what practices they would require, they became a philosophic compass for the first few years.

The Early Days

On the evening of September 23, 1996, we launched JAS anticipating that we would open the door and see what happened.

With reciprocity as the guiding principle, we trusted people would teach us what they wanted to learn, and we would do like-

JAS children, performing a play, use masks of Jane Addams.

wise. Crowded into a small room in the Neighborhood House settlement on the West Side of St. Paul, a handful of college students, a few faculty, 12 Hmong people (mostly women) along with several native Spanish speakers, began to craft what and how people wanted to learn together. We developed a format using a learning-circle method adapted from the Highlander model. Each learning circle held a 30-minute "cultural exchange," carried on in three languages, followed by self-directed study in learning pairs. Two bilingual college students, who spoke Hmong and Spanish, served as interpreters.[6]

The Hmong women were reluctant to speak in either language, embarrassed by their lack of English skill and uncertain about the expectations of this new school. They did, however, express urgency in needing to learn the English answers on the U.S. citizenship test before taking it. With the 1996 Welfare Reform Act about to be enacted, the women would lose their government assistance if they remained noncitizens. Thus, while many of us had imagined working together on dramatic sociopolitical change efforts, we instead set goals for teaching and learning the 100 history and civics questions on the citizenship test. We didn't immediately see the social

and political significance of hundreds of Hmong refugees becoming citizens. We had a lot to learn!

As that first night progressed, we realized that many Hmong adults were unable to read or write in any language, because Hmong is a relatively new written language and few adults had attended formal school. Not one among us had ever taught a language. College students and faculty were overwhelmed with the seeming impossibility of communicating without a common language and with the enormity of the challenge to learn the questions and answers in English. We realized we were all embarking on a steep learning curve. By the end of the first evening, we had

achieved two things: We could say, "My name is" in Hmong and English; and the Hmong people had learned to say and read *cit*, the first syllable of the word *citizen*. It wasn't a lot, but we felt an undeniable sense of individual and collective possibility.

Ten years later, more than 1500 participants at JAS—Hmong, East Africans, and Latin Americans—have become citizens. In retrospect, participants at JAS have accomplished far more than passing the citizenship test. Our work with the late Senator Paul Wellstone and the late Representative Bruce Vento led to legislation that recognized Hmong veterans of the Vietnam War and allowed them and their spouses to take the citizenship test in Hmong. We partnered with the local district director of the U.S. Citizenship and Immigration Services (USCIS) on legislative work and policy reform resulting from that legislation. We negotiated a policy change that allows for a nonparticipant observer to be present while the citizenship test is administered. This partnership opened communication between the district USCIS and local immigrant communities and led to JAS involvement in the current citi-

zenship redesign effort. We have pioneered a multilingual discussion format for candidate forums during mayoral and school-board elections that improves the quality of dialogue between candidates and citizens. (In these forums, candidates rotate among small assemblies of people grouped according to languages spoken, with each group using an interpreter. Participants discuss issues of concern ahead of time, gather background information, and prepare questions for the candidates.) In 2000 when Minnesota's Mee Moua became the first Hmong state senator in the United States, it became evident that gaining citizenship *is* about social change.

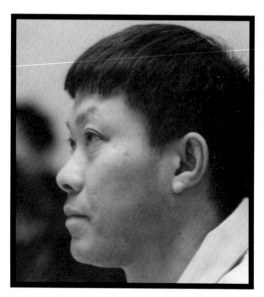

Growth of the Learning Circles

We soon recognized the awkwardness in translating conversation into three languages. Although we concluded learning would be more effective in two languages, given the short amount of time together in each session, we held to the ideal that JAS could create a learning space across multiple cultures. Thus, separate Spanish-speaking and Hmong circles formed early on, with a commitment to establish regular occasions for everyone at JAS to interact. These frequent gatherings and celebrations have helped bind people together across differences in class, culture, and age.

In the first years, the Hmong Circle grew exponentially through word of mouth, due in part to a laser-like focus on gaining citizenship status. Members of the Spanish-Speaking Circle did not have this same sense of urgency about citizenship, and the group, which met only one evening each week was smaller. This eclectic, but tightly knit little group of Spanish speakers began with two Mexican grandmothers, several young Latin American men who wanted to improve English skills

See Moua (left) helps Hmong immigrants study for their citizenship test. Here she explains the symbolism of the stars and stripes in the American flag.

for their work in local restaurants, and an English-speaking neighbor and college students who wanted to practice their language skills with native Spanish speakers. As in the Hmong Circle, long-term friendships formed and continue even though some members have moved back to their countries of origin. Over the years many U.S. natives have visited Latin American friends formed in the Spanish-Speaking Circle. People who participate at JAS say that the opportunity to form friendships across cultures is one of its most valued outcomes.

One long-time member, who joined as a college student and continues four years later, put it like this:

> There are few places if any, in my life where I can develop relationships with such a diverse group of people in age, ethnicity, and backgrounds. When people enter the circle on Wednesday nights, we remove all titles and labels. We are who we are. In this space, people have a sense of equality. Because we have such different lived experiences, everyone brings a needed perspective. This matters in a democracy. We

have to be able to come into dialogue knowing how to tell our stories to others, to be able to say what we believe and why, and to hear each other's stories. . . . JAS teaches us how. [At JAS] people assume there is a valid story to tell, which is different from expectations experienced in most places.[7]

An East African Circle and multiple children and teen groups emanating from the Children's Circle have expanded the school. In the adult circles, we begin with a public discussion on a topic of interest to the group. Topics range broadly from discussion of upcoming elections to issues of global concern to exchanges about cultural traditions, such as dating, marriage, clothing, and child rearing. These circle discussions provide a forum for JAS members to share ideas and cultural knowledge. After 30 minutes of large-group conversation, participants work in learning pairs or small groups. On a typical evening, members who have become citizens might work in a reading group or organize for political action around a large issue; others might help college students with class projects and papers related to immigration or cultural traditions. Together,

we have created a place where people can redefine roles, norms, and ways of being together across differences that become part of the reward and challenge of the relationships.

Shortly after JAS began, we realized the need for a children's circle. The challenge was to create it in a way that embodied the JAS philosophy. Guided by the spirit and insights of Aleida Benitez, a University of Minnesota student, the circle grew into a space where children could explore their interests and pursue their ideas. Within a year, about 60 children and young teens speaking a variety of languages, verbal and nonverbal, participated in the circle along with their college-student learning partners. Children have taught each other and all of us to laugh, to listen, and to learn large lessons from small projects. Their creative energy and surprising conviction remind adults to hope as they urge us to respond to our own public passions.

We have learned that children and young people take public issues seriously. They worry about their parents' ability to pass the citizenship test in English and write letters to legislators. They work on school-reform issues

and help their siblings with homework and language issues. They have helped all of us understand the importance of multiage relationships.

Although it would take time to understand the complexities and tensions in working across cultures and generations, it became clear that public places should be intergenerational spaces as well. Intergenerational discussions help young people see the value of maintaining cultural roots in new contexts. Unfortunately, the dominant culture can persuade immigrants to dissolve their cultural histories in the great American "melting pot." Thus, immigrant children too easily forget the language, values, dreams, and contributions of their elders. We intended that JAS members would follow a different path. Indeed, the story of JAS is told by a growing chorus of young voices that say: *We are making this place together. We know who we are, where we've been, and we will honor our heritage and those who have given it to us.*

The West Side

We found a home in St. Paul's West Side neighborhood, a portal of entry for new immigrants since the mid-nineteenth century.

Because the West Side is a discrete neighborhood, bounded on three sides by the Mississippi River and on the fourth by a county line, West Siders have always had a clear sense of place unlike residents in many contiguous urban neighborhoods that run one into another without such defining boundaries. About 16,000 people live in this culturally diverse neighborhood, with new immigrant families residing in three public housing projects on the lower West Side. Visitors are struck by the abundance of public art—exquisite murals and sculptures—depicting West Side history and the ethnic stories of groups who've made their home there. From the beginning, we knew the neighborhood would be an integral part of the learning community we intended to build, offering a specific geographic location that embodied both the challenges and opportunities that come with a diverse public setting.

The importance of the 100-year-old West Side settlement as one of the original supporting institutions cannot be understated. Sandy Fuller, then program director at Neighborhood House,

helped us make connections with leaders in the Hmong and Latino communities so that we could engage a broader group of people in the JAS planning process. Sandy saw her interests embedded in the idea of JAS. "Settlement houses are now more akin to social service agencies

The Mississippi River and downtown St. Paul viewed from the West Side

than places for civic empowerment," she reflected in an early conversation. She was interested in the ideas of public work and democratic education and wanted to help Neighborhood House staff reclaim an older settlement mission. Neighborhood House provided an incubation space that allowed JAS to take form.

Institutional Relationships

JAS began with three supporting institutions in the Twin Cities: Neighborhood House, the College of St. Catherine, and the University of Minnesota (particularly, the Center for Democracy and Citizenship at the Humphrey Institute of Public Affairs and the College of Liberal Arts). The evolution of these relationships yields lessons about places for experimentation connected with, but not governed or owned by, any one institution.[8] For instance, the faculty at the College of St. Catherine had redesigned the core curriculum and wanted to experiment with a more active, student-centered pedagogy. Frustrated by the structures that organize and constrain reform in higher education, faculty and student leaders sought opportunities free of these structures to develop practices in active learning. JAS provided an alternative learning environment for students and faculty. Likewise Neighborhood House leaders wanted an opportunity to experiment with the recovery and potential adaptation

of earlier, more democratic practices of settlement work to their current model. In these ways, the supporting institutions could invest resources and energy in the enterprise, observe what could happen with alternative structures, claim and implement its innovations, and, we hoped, reform the institution from the margins. There is some evidence that this is happening. For instance, the University of Minnesota launched a civic mission initiative with the broad purpose of rebuilding its institutional civic culture and land-grant tradition. One facet of that work seeks

to identify and understand the dynamics of reciprocal community relationships in addressing public problems. The university names its partnership with JAS as one successful model of institutional civic engagement and effective community-based learning for students.

JAS is not a 501(c)(3) organization; it exists within the "parentheses" of a network of supporting organizations that relate more directly to JAS than they do to each other. This structure proved an effective way for JAS to maintain accountability to the community, to foundations,

and to its collaborating institutions, while ensuring creativity and shared ownership. The arrangement provides greater flexibility for fiscal administration while allowing JAS to link into existing institutional infrastructure like budget systems, human resources, and technology, without having to carry the full cost of developing and maintaining its own infrastructure.

Building and sustaining relationships among four organizations, three of which are not located in the West Side neighborhood, was challenging work. From the beginning, we anticipated the potential for negative impact, which can occur when large institutions attempt work in communities; consequently we refrained from "leading" with college and university connections, though we have been able to broker many resources for JAS and the West Side neighborhood in the last decade.

The level of investment among the original founding organizations has shifted over the years. The strength of individual connections with home institutions and the ability to build networks and broker resources has been a factor affecting the level of investment by any one institution. As JAS leaders have moved out of key roles at the College of St. Catherine and Neighborhood House, these organizations' relationships with us have weakened somewhat, although some shared work continues. In time, other neighborhood organizations and colleges have stepped in, while the university's involvement, especially through the Humphrey Institute's Center for Democracy and Citizenship, remains strong. We recognize the benefits that accrue from the involvement of multiple organizations and continue to seek ways to grow the network of relationships, particularly with local colleges.

The early traditions and ideas of the community settlement house inspired the philosophy of JAS. The use of Neighborhood House space provided a central location and legitimacy for the "new kids on the block." In short, Neighborhood House offered an essential incubation space. As time went on and JAS grew in numbers, differences in organizational purposes and structures produced tensions that both groups struggled to resolve. JAS leaders saw their work as pushing against bureaucratic

constraints to open spaces where people could express creativity and develop civic identities. Nonprofit organizations like Neighborhood House focus on serving clients' needs. Especially in an environment of growing competition for resources, they define their work as creating structures that facilitate efficient, effective program delivery, and they often adopt business models that do not easily accommodate the messy democratic work of neighborhoods. In addition there is an acceptance of limited flexibility. These fundamental differences in structure and organizational culture complicated collaboration between JAS and Neighborhood House. By 2002, JAS felt the limits of physical space and bureaucratic constraints and relocated to the neighborhood public high school.

Radical Roots

In hindsight, we see our beginnings in radical terms. In the face of conventional wisdom about program development and grant seeking, we resisted the urge to predict a set of outcomes, preferring "to make the road by walking," as Myles Horton once advised. Partly because of this, we

did not rely on foundation funding for the first two years. Many of us had years of experience with foundation accountability structures that were predicated on measurable outcomes, organizational governance structures, and staff/volunteer job descriptions. We believed that to create a democratic organization, responsive to and reflective of participant interests, organizational structures and projects should not be predetermined. It was profoundly liberating to cultivate an organization that emerged organically from practice. We insisted that we could learn from one another and that there were resources and creative talents among the participants to accomplish our goals. Thus we kept options open rather than developing the plan first and subsequently learned that, when environments are open to possibility and guided by a clear vision, people move forward with imagination. This belief remains part of the JAS ethos.

The rise of expert knowledge and the socialization of the professional class has shaped public problem solving in profound and complicated ways. The default tendency to assign

Core Commitments

Central to these underlying ideas are a set of core "commitments," sometimes expressed as values, beliefs, or simply, JAS practices. Combined, they serve as the compass that keeps the organization on its course.

Embrace difference. Koshin Ahmed explains in his interview, "A Civic Community," that diversity makes differences visible. "When you learn what you are not, you realize who you are." Learning to accept difference is a first step. To recognize its value and necessity for a democratic society is a second and perhaps more challenging task. Yet it remains a question central to a flourishing public life: how do diverse individuals become a "we"?

An exchange between Terri Wilson, who in 1997 was a college sophomore from a small town in Wisconsin, and See Vang, a 35-year-old widow and Hmong refugee with a large family of children, who arrived in the United States in the 1980s, helps illustrate typical interactions at JAS between people of very different lived experiences.

One night, See reached across the table to Terri and with the help of a bilingual speaker shared her powerful story of the harrowing crossing of the Mekong River into Thailand. (See her narrative, "The Journey.") Terri recorded her reaction in a journal entry:

> these broken glass events
> ease off of her too smoothly.
> i want to fill the spaces between
> me and her, between her words
> and downward glances, between
> that place & time and this
> with anger—something heavy
> and solid and flat.
> i want to be water or rage...
> some action besides this slow
> silence and paralysis of beaten
> down emotion and empathy.
> (she doesn't wear me down...the
> story—its delicate neutrality
> erodes me away...so that I slump
> down & cannot speak.)

Terri's ability to bear witness to See's experience and See's acceptance of Terri's response reveals a reciprocity that allows the development of relationships across what would otherwise be very different worlds. In this example, difference became part of the joy in their long-lasting relationship. Embracing difference is an enormous challenge—for many a lifelong pursuit. It requires a spirit of generosity to listen fully to another while suspending judgment or interpretation. Storytelling and story listening are part of the pedagogy for learning reciprocal interaction. It takes time, but the process holds potential for extraordinary personal reward. When this occurs in public settings, it affirms that people can work together *with*, not in spite of, differences.

Reach for understanding. It became immediately clear as JAS took shape that the familiar academic and professional ways of knowing from the "outside-in"—processes that favor objective, disciplinary knowing—excluded important and legitimate sources of knowledge. Partly out of necessity and in part reflecting our desire to explore "wholehearted learning," as Parker Palmer calls it, we created a way of working grounded in more holistic learning. It takes patience and skill to appreciate this way of knowing. Learning to listen with the ear *and* the heart is not the dominant way in Western society. It requires suspension of judgment about meaning and value and the ability to dig deep to understand the experience as told and lived by another. People who remain at JAS over a period of time tend to be those most interested and appreciative of this kind of reciprocity and its mysteries. Kathleen Winters, in her essay, "The Language of Learning," describes a wholehearted communication process she and her partner discovered through contextual, reciprocal teaching and learning.

We recognized early that we could not realize our mantra that "everyone is a teacher and a learner" if all conversation happened in English. Traditional English Language Learning (ELL) programs encourage the "everything in English" approach:

Repeat after me . . . write these words that I put on the board. . . and gradually you will learn how to use the words in a sentence. While helpful as a language-learning approach, for many people it also implies that English learners cannot communicate until they have grasped adequate English. Perhaps out of impatience, JAS sought a complementary alternative.

Because we did not want to hamper our commitment to understanding the meaning each person gave to the pattern of events and issues in their lives, we began to develop a fluid practice of oral translation. Initially we focused on translation of

Learning partners Sandy Fuller (left) and Va Lee

simple words, such as *my name is
. . .* or *Kuv lub npe*, with everyone
participating in the exchange,
English and non-English speakers
alike. But quickly people began to
seek other ways to translate their
questions, their worries, their
basic human need to be known
and to know another. Bilingual
students (college and high school)
began to develop roles as translators. In addition to language
translation, students also helped
with cultural interpretation as
they strengthened their own ability to speak fluently in their native
languages. Immigrant elders
thus became their mentors, often
correcting mispronunciations
or helping to expand students'
limited vocabularies.

Translation at JAS grew into a
multilevel activity understood
both as a practice and metaphor
for mutual understanding. All of
us "tuned" our ears. We learned
to listen to tone, to nonverbal
cues in the narratives, as well as
to the interpreter's chosen words.
English speakers acquired the
ability to understand English
spoken with Hmong and Somali
accents. Interestingly, this level of
attentiveness revealed new ideas
about other kinds of translation
and its relevance to the multiple

languages found in diverse cultures of the academy, government,
and nonprofit settings, as well as
street cultures. Thus, the commitment to reach understanding
has come to mean finding ways
to actively meet "an other" across
language, age, and culture of kind.

Practice democracy. We quickly
discovered a striking dissonance
between the JAS philosophy and
the conventional wisdom that
people need to accept "what is."
Indeed entrenched professionalized practices represent the
fact that many believe them
unchangeable—"It's just the way
it is." For instance, nonprofit

organizations recruit college students as volunteers but rarely
see them as helping to shape their
missions. Most nonprofits that
offer student internships provide
social-service programs that focus
on client needs rather than building their clients' capacity for civic
agency. In the academy, while
colleges have embraced the idea
of service learning tied to course
work, they have not dealt with
the structural limitations to sustained work in the community.
Foundations want to partner with
organizations in ways more colle-
gial and reflective of local cultural
groups, but they expect hierarchi-

cal management structures that include boards of directors, executive directors, staff, volunteers—structures often out of sync with non-Western and indigenous groups. While many professionals believe that new immigrants have much to contribute to the community and schools, the everyday reality of institutional practices marginalizes immigrant cultures and languages.

JAS participants have worked with stubborn determination to cocreate new possibilities—new ways of moving beyond the idea of a fixed reality toward new possibilities jointly imagined. Because we work in spaces between and among sponsoring institutions, JAS has been able to experiment in innovative ways—as we would not likely have been able to do had we been owned by, or embedded in, any one organization. The expectation that people can create new options freed us and cultivated the talents among us all—including the children.

It was the children who helped us understand what we didn't want to do: reproduce a daycare model or a formal school setting. We started from the belief that children could teach us and we could learn from them. They were growing up in large families with siblings of many ages. Therefore, it made sense to build on their experiences of cross-age learning. The children spoke many languages, including the nonverbal languages of imagination, play, and music, as well as Hmong, Spanish, Somali, and English. How could we learn from each other if we could not understand each other? It was both a dilemma and, as it turns out, our opportunity.

Aleida Benitez, a talented listener to children in their multiple languages, guided the Children's Circle in the early years, never allowing people to limit themselves by the status quo. In 1999, Aleida and a group of eight girls worried about their parents' struggles with the citizenship test and imagined they could talk with the Minnesota congressional delegation in Washington, D.C., to discuss their parents' concerns. Few adults thought the trip possible—the girls were young, the cost was high, and Hmong girls rarely left home without family. After many months of car washes, egg-roll sales, and various community fundraisers, they raised $7,000—enough to cover expenses. They met with Minnesota senators and representatives, received useful press coverage, and later helped contribute to a national redesign of the U.S. citizenship test.

The efforts of the girls of the Earth Day Club, now part of the JAS legacy, had long-lasting effects. Most important, we discovered in the midst of the work that we *were* creating an alternative to the childcare model. And the adults and children worked it out together. This and other lessons learned along the way have contributed to the commitment that we will not limit possibility.

Through the ordinary experience of work at JAS, individuals and small groups began to internalize the liberating idea that they were *doing* democracy—working together in new ways, taking on large challenges, interacting with policymakers at all levels. People came to appreciate the notion that citizenship means more than legal status. Eduardo Jurado, an immigrant from Peru, describes this in his essay, "Bridging the Americas." Unable to apply for citizenship for many years has not limited his civic work or his deep appreciation of democracy. He tells us:

Shao Lee gave a party to celebrate becoming a U.S. citizen. Here she is shown with some of the food she cooked for 100 guests at JAS.

In my country you pay a fine if you don't vote, and you will not be allowed to hold a government job until the fine is paid. Here people inherit this wonderful democracy and many don't bother to vote . . . . So promoting democracy for those who are indifferent is crucial, especially at this time when citizens need to assume responsibility and power. Right now I am not allowed to vote [in the U.S.], but I'm happy to help other people prepare for voting through education.

Over the last years, we have grappled with the deeper meanings of the nation's core democratic values. Those living in the United States the longest often explain to the newcomers how to engage in public life; they share interpretations of the political landscape and discuss general expectations of citizenship. In exchange, newcomers share their understandings and passion for freedom and the rewards of work for the common good. We hear firsthand the results of the loss of civil liberties and harsh realities of life under dictatorships.

Public work is the venue through which people practice democracy and act as cocreators of a communal life. Many of these principles share similarities with the Hmong clan system or the indigenous Latino and African cultural groups. What struck us most forcibly was the clarity and seemingly higher value many new immigrants place on the ideals of freedom and democracy: for them the ideas are attainable, tangible, and worth risking everything.

Learning to "walk the talk" is a continual process of acting and reflecting on the patterns of behaviors. Do the actions match the intended purpose and values of the organization? What do the commitments look like in concrete terms? At JAS, these conversations are part of our core work. In this way participants cocreate the philosophy through circular processes of acting, learning, reflecting, and making meaning of it all. A lived philosophy is visible, often challenged, and continually developing; it does not happen passively or without tension; it requires tolerance for confusion and disorder. It is in the productive give and take around large ideas, however, that we stretch and find ways to open to other points of view. In the process, we practice democracy.

On the Other Side of the Window

By Nan Skelton

In the summer of 1980, sitting in my sunroom in an overstuffed reading chair, I watched the daily procession of Hmong refugees, as they walked past our house on the way to fish on Lake Phalen. They were dressed in multipatterned, out-of-season, too-big clothing donated from church rummage sales. Little children, packed with energy, but uncommonly tentative, followed behind the lead elders whose lived age was much beyond their birth age. I'd read newspaper reports of "the boat people" who were resettling in St. Paul and felt unusually strange as I suspected the horrors they had traveled before making the trek to Lake Phalen. I sat on the other side of the window, wishing I could come out, could speak with them and yet, I was too frightened to do so.

Seventeen years later I am seated in a hot, too-small room as we, at the Jane Addams School, host a dialogue with Senator Paul Wellstone, Congressman Bruce Vento, and 300 Hmong adults. We listen to former soldiers, mothers, wives, and daughters tell their stories of rescuing American pilots, nursing them back to health, fleeing their villages after the U.S. military pulled out, trekking through the night jungle with 30 to 40 family members. Women, containing their grief no longer, cried out for the babies shot off their backs. I cried, too. While they were fleeing their villages, I was here harboring the agony of seeing my country engaged in something so wrong. I was now with them on the other side of the window.

PUBLIC WORK: A PRACTICAL THEORY

by Nan Kari

In the early 1990s, I was a professor in the field of occupational therapy struggling with how health professions and higher education might liberate and develop their democratic possibilities. The profession of occupational therapy originated with the idea that meaningful work could contribute to human health and well-being. In recent decades, however, these larger insights were eclipsed by more reductionist ways of thinking about human function.

I felt this shift was symptomatic of many professions, which had come to rely on specialized knowledge and techniques. In a quest to better understand how professionals might rethink their everyday work in more democratic, interactive ways, I joined with colleagues affiliated with Project Public Life at the Humphrey Institute of Public Affairs to help develop a practical political theory that expanded the meaning of citizenship.[1] Building on this work, in 1996, Harry Boyte and I authored *Building America: The Democratic Promise of Public Work*, which analyzed practical democratic experiments both local and national, to critique conventional ideas of citizenship and public life.[2] We proposed a practical political theory based on the concept of work as a potential source of democratic power. From its beginnings, the Jane Addams School for Democracy became a laboratory to better understand the core ideas and practices of public work, a practical theory of democracy.

Public work theory emphasizes the capacity of work and work environments to generate civic learning and to create public cultures. Put most simply, public work is defined as the visible, sustained efforts of a diverse mix of people that produce goods—material or cultural—of lasting civic value. Citizens are thus cocreators and producers, not only bearers of rights and responsible members of communities. Public work points to the *productive* not just the *distributive* side of politics, thus defining politics as about creating and building communities and, more broadly, as a democratic way of life.

The Roots of Public Work

The historical roots of public work and its contribution to the renewal of democratic life in the United States influenced our initial thinking about the purposes and potential of the Jane Addams School. In the nineteenthth century, Hull offered a remarkable example: ordinary people—many of them immigrants—were able to address large issues affecting their lives. With a longstanding concern for the welfare of children, for example, residents at Hull House organized a kindergarten and established the first public playground in Chicago. They stood in strong support of the creation of the first juvenile court in the nation—a needed alternative to the criminal court. In contrast, the juvenile judge was expected to rule with an understanding of the interests and developmental needs of young people. Hull House, with its direct link to the national settlement movement, thus became an important social-reform organization, helping local people influence public policy on many fronts, labor reform among them. Public work was central to achieving significant social reform in Chicago and to influencing policy change at the city, state, and federal levels.

Hull House was also an incubator for women leaders active in social reform. The boldness of the vision and inventiveness of that environment drew and nurtured remarkable women who organized others to achieve significant social change. Florence Kelly spearheaded reform in the garment industry and helped form the National Consumer's League; Julia Lathrop, influenced policies that humanized treatment of people with mental illnesses; Ellen Gates Starr, a cofounder of Hull House, moved an agenda that promoted education and welfare of young children; and Alice Hamilton, a medical doctor drawn to the activities at Hull House, helped pressure politicians to develop workmen's compensation laws and standards for safer working conditions. These women and others affiliated with the settlement movement left an inspiring legacy that helped us begin to imagine a settlement tradition reinvented for the twenty-first century.

Like the settlement example of the early twentieth century, much of the public work that occurred historically in this country generated what were called "mediating institutions," rooted in local areas yet able to connect people to larger worlds of policy and politics. Such mediating institutions educated citizens in political skills and habits and also generated civic muscle for larger action.[3] Through the 1940s and into the 1950s in American society, these institutions existed in abundance—churches and synagogues, voluntary groups, community centers, settlement houses, newspapers, schools, political parties, trade unions, and the like. They formed the heart of popular democratic politics and a dynamic understanding of democracy as a way of life. These "people's organizations" were places where people developed a sense of ownership in public life, shaped agendas, developed political skills, and addressed issues of common concern. Because they often belonged to large national networks, these connections could be used to broker power and raise public visibility of issues. The net effect of these many political activities created a public culture far more vibrant than we currently see.

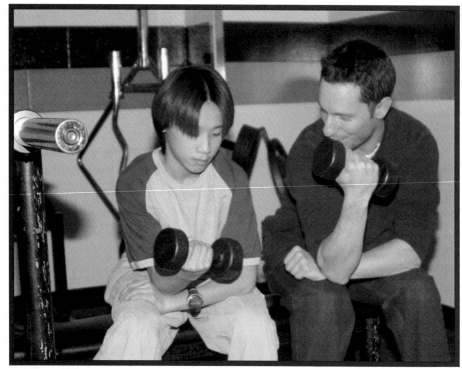

Teenaged boys at JAS organized a small work project, which resulted in a successful proposal to the principal of Humboldt High School. Their aim was to get permission to use the school's fitness center, originally off-limits to JAS students. Tong Vang (left) works in the school fitness center with trainer Jess Bauer.

Over time this mediating function eroded. In particular, the growth of professional classes became increasingly self-referential subcultures, detached from the civic life of places and thus the reciprocal, interactive relationships with other citizens. This "necessary" detachment of the "outside expert," thought to be at the center of problem solving, favored disciplinary knowledge. Thus ordinary, "uncredentialed" people were conceived as clients —needy, deficient, and reliant on experts in everything from child rearing to education. As civic missions, public practices, and the civic identities of professionals faded, public-spirited institutions, such as schools, settlements, unions, YWCAs and YMCAs, gradually lost their civic dimensions. Our society's trajectory toward privatization in every aspect of the public world can be seen as the logical culmination of this dynamic.

Today, democratic governance has given way to a bureaucratic, corporate model in which citizens are reconceived as consumers to be entertained and left to their private worlds. Elected officials manipulate information to mold messages that "sell" rather than working with citizens to determine solutions. Too often public officials seek to insulate their actions from public scrutiny. The collective loss of citizen agency compounded by the disappearance of public places where people hone public skills, both reflect and magnify the crisis in our society.

Public Work Theory

When work acquires public meanings, it enriches our understanding of democracy and holds potential for generating new authority and power for ordinary people in several distinctive ways. Work with visible impact done "in public," can enhance the claims of citizens to full and *equal participation* in public life as we saw in the women's movement of the 1960s and 1970s. In this sense, public work is a central strategy for social, racial, and economic justice. Second, the products of public work—or work that creates public things—helps to *build the public world*. Through that work, people create multiple connections to the public world—now in danger of becoming considerably less public as people have lost a sense of their own role in its creation and sustenance. Finally, work of the public, involving diverse people and groups who learn how to negotiate and work together for larger ends, *educates citizens*. In the process, public work can illuminate local cultures, which in turn helps to sustain such work.

The bold premise of the public work framework is that it can reverse the dynamics eroding democracy. Public work focuses on what public things are created, what new patterns of relationships form, what new public habits and skills are developed, and what normative and cultural changes are needed to sustain such work and civic agency. Simply put, public work, in recovering the public dimensions of serious work—within neighborhoods and in work places among blue-collar workers, corporate leaders, academics, and professionals—holds potential for

educating people for effective, confident, and productive citizenship while it also works larger culture change in institutions and society. The renewal of the civic dimension of worker identities and practices can interact with the recovery of the public missions of institutions in a mutually reinforcing dynamic. This theoretical conception of work and its potential for democratic renewal undergird our thinking and practices at the Jane Addams School.

A Catalyst of Public Work

The creation of JAS occurred against a backdrop worth noting. Leaders in higher education, some echoing their students' critique, were increasingly raising the issue of the disconnect between disciplinary research and the complicated problems that communities actually face. Concerns with the decline in civic participation among college-aged students had spurred the creation of new task forces and revised agendas in many national higher education associations. At the state level in Minnesota, media attention had focused on a growing demographic diversity with the arrival of new immigrant

groups whose cultures were distinctly different from earlier arrivals of European heritage.[4] In St. Paul, for instance, children speaking 83 different languages and dialects had enrolled in public schools in 1996-1997, a dramatic change over a relatively short period of time.[5] These trends shaped the public work taken up by people at JAS.

In ten years, JAS members have engaged in several major public work efforts with significant positive outcomes—helping to pass the Hmong Veterans Bill; building a relationship with the district Immigration and Naturalization Service that resulted in the formation of new policy, contribution to the redesign of the U.S. citizenship test; and helping to conceptualize efforts to renew the land-grant mission at the University of Minnesota. JAS has opened public space for debate and organizing, built networks, brokered resources, and supported the leadership development of many people, both immigrants and U.S.-born citizens.

Early on, JAS participants struggled to find ways to influence their children's education. In 2001, JAS clarified an agenda to improve learning for children through community improvement and education reform that involved a radical shift in agency: Schools alone cannot educate children; the whole community is responsible. Along with several other West Side organizations, JAS leaders launched an initiative called the Neighborhood Learning Community (NLC), which incorporates a public work philosophy based on the idea of shared responsibility for the education of children across an entire neighborhood.

The NLC has built a network of community businesses, nonprofits, and individual residents to cocreate a culture of learning in the neighborhood. It is essentially an organizing initiative that has increased citizen involvement in public-school issues, heightened visibility of learning experiences in nonschool settings, deepened many groups' connections to the neighborhood and each other, and has begun to establish useable pathways between the community and its schools.

After five years, more than 2,000 children, youth, and adults have engaged in innovative neighborhood-based learning opportunities, often designed and led by parents. For example, the West Side organized a free neighborhood trolley, or bus, that circulates regularly throughout the neighborhood during the summer and after school throughout the year to connect children and adults with learning sites in the community. This is particularly significant because the city does not have public transportation designed specifically to meet the needs of individual neighborhoods.

Parents working with educators helped design and participate in professional development seminars to learn how to present projects in a way that animates children's curiosity and uses the neighborhood as an important site of learning. This self-development effort, inspired by the Reggio Emilia approach to democratic education has sparked the beginnings of a neighborhood-based education institute to prepare parents and other neighborhood adults to lead an innovative after-school and summer program for children.[6] Parents and other neighborhood residents who participate in seminars teach in All-Around-the Neighborhood, a project-based series of learning opportunities designed to help children and youth build connections with places and people in the community.

In a related project, teens have roles as paid apprentices in neighborhood businesses and nonprofit organizations. More than 30 adults have mentored neighborhood youth as they explored career interests and experienced public contribution through work, in the West Side Youth Apprenticeship Project. These and other neighborhood generated and owned projects are tangible efforts that generate a power base for larger organizing work focused on school reform.

When public-school administrators denied the use of school buildings for All-Around-the-Neighborhood camps in the summer of 2005, a citizen-led group persuaded high-level administrators and school-board members in the St. Paul public school district to collaborate with West Side leaders to address the troubling cultural and relational gap between schools and neighborhoods. Organizations supporting the NLC had built sufficient political clout to influence public-school officials to form a partnership whose goals were to better align school sys-

St. Paul Public Schools superintendent Patricia Harvey at a meeting organized by Plua Ly at her home

tems with community resources and to create a model that could be expanded to other neighborhoods. Relationships with the new mayor and buy-in with his agenda to promote out-of-school learning in a citywide initiative he calls The Second Shift has also catapulted the work from the neighborhood to a broader arena. Thus, as West Siders engage in work to build a different neighborhood culture, they have come to see themselves as civic actors, people able to take on large issues and capable of shaping the community and improving education for children.

JAS, functioning as a mediating institution in the spirit of early settlements, provided the space for participants to set a public agenda. JAS worked with other organizations to convene public dialogue and eventually to launch the NLC initiative. The JAS relationships with public leaders at the city, state, and national levels, developed over ten years, have leveraged funding and other important resources that support the ongoing work in the neighborhood and beyond. JAS also continues as a place of leadership development for immigrant adults, youth, and college students, many of whom lead efforts in education reform.

Early JAS organizers had faith in a compelling vision, a collective passion and fierce determination that we could build a culture of democratic work together with the new immigrants arriving in St. Paul. In retrospect, ragged though the beginnings may have been, it was the large vision that motivated this eclectic group. We relied on collective experiences and shared insights to generate a set of principles and practices that would transform lives well beyond the walls of that "one" room. The importance of public passion and large ideas cannot be underrated in this experience of public work.

Several interrelated ideas characterize public work as it has deepened through the experiences at JAS: the process of co-learning; importance of the particularities of context; and its capacity to renew public cultures.

Co-learning

Public work implies a particular kind of learning, one that embraces an open-ended, collaborative inquiry process that contrasts sharply with the patterns of tightly scripted roles and outcome driven action predominant in school systems. It is also distinctive from the approach to learning in bureaucratic systems where outputs and outcomes are predetermined. In contrast, learning associated with public work involves the co-construction of knowledge from multiple sources —lived experience, disciplinary knowledge from academic fields, as well as cultural knowledge. As a college professor who felt trapped by the confines of class schedules with learning chunked into semesters and strong focus on disciplinary knowing, I have felt both liberated and fascinated with the impact of wholehearted learning that acknowledges the fullness of the learner's experience.

JAS offers a learning community of the richest kind. With the conviction that learning is political, people take up the most important issues, examine personal bias, look at familiar situations through alternative lenses, and, in the process, challenge old ways of thinking and being. For many students, the JAS environment offers a poignant contrast to the more familiar classroom-centered experience. Sara Carpenter, who in 2001 was a senior at Macalester College, described her experience in this way:

> People like me can be blabber-mouth college students who think they have answers because we read something in a book. The space at JAS asks you to consider what other people are saying—to consider other voices, others' knowledge, whether from books, theory, or experience—as legitimate sources. I learned to take up the role as listener, which required me to also examine my role as talker. The two [roles] need to engage each other. Before coming to JAS, when I would have conversations with people in student groups at school, it seemed more like a listening–talking exercise where you would argue your point without listening too much to what others were saying, except to find the flaw in their argument. This meant we kept saying the same thing over and over again. What others said didn't have much impact on me.
>
> At JAS, because we have to listen so hard to really hear what others say, arguments can change . . . and it has become easier for me to let it happen, to admit I'm wrong about something without seeing it as a bad thing. This is learning. If you're going to learn something new, then you have to be willing to change your mind about it. It is also a political skill.[7]

Such learning invites serious engagement and sometimes, playful encounters that can turn old ways upside down. In her essay, "Children Teach Us," See

Moua explains how a democratic learning environment profoundly shaped her way of seeing children's abilities and their contributions as teachers and learners. When children learn to work in groups, to encounter situations from multiple angles, to give and take in their problem-solving processes, to experiment with new ways of doing things they, like adults, are learning the fundamentals of democratic participation.

To engage in active learning implies an ongoing process of meaning making—a powerful intellectual activity bound together with the public product it creates. The JAS Freedom Festival offers a simple example. Each summer JAS members organize a neighborhood celebration in the spirit of old-fashioned small-town gatherings. This annual multicultural neighborhood festival honors new citizens, as well as children, who have made contributions to the community during the past year. People look forward to the wonderful array of ethnic foods, the colorful traditional clothing from many parts of the world, the music, dancing, games, and mostly, the lively conversation. To avoid

Hmong mothers help their daughters dress in traditional costumes for a dance performance at the JAS Freedom Festival.

the commercialization of typical community fairs, we neither sell nor buy anything. We eat our potluck banquet.

In 2005, as festival organizers put plans in place, we raised some of the questions we regularly discussed. We had an idea that

Two Hmong participants and three East African boys share potluck dishes at the Freedom Festival.

how to engage diversity? How do college students experience the event? What does freedom mean?

The day after the event, gathered around a computer with a slide show of photos taken at the festival and short quotations collected from participants, the group worked to understand the fuller meaning of the experience. We focused especially on how people cross cultural borders to create a diverse public. One Somali man reflected:

> Coming from a homogeneous community, the Freedom Festival is a powerful experience for me. It brings hope that very diverse people can come together without rigid rules. It makes me think that we can learn to live together peacefully. The Freedom Festival honors new citizens, but it also helps amplify . . . the importance of belonging to a larger community.

We continued our study of the photographs and interviews in a later retreat session, where we honed other questions to pursue over the course of the next year. This meaning-making process, when political concepts are explicit, encourages democratic practices. It invites multiple points of view. It opens new ways of seeing. It asks people to

we could study them through documentation of the festival experience. How do people cross cultural borders? What are the access points? Does the potluck serve a purpose other than providing a meal? What does it mean to wear the traditional clothing of another's culture? What roles do children play in showing others become philosophers of everyday life, and in so doing, to imagine a common life built together. In this way, public work offers a powerful antidote to our market-driven society, which insidiously convinces us that we are consumers, not producers of ideas and new knowledge.

The Importance of Narrative

America today, driven by market language of the "bottom line," by values of individual competitive success, celebrity personality, and an ever-expanding private world of consumer choices, reveals a profound loss of public memory and common knowledge of what it takes to build thriving communities. The textures and rhythms of daily life, the smells and sounds of unique places, the slower pace that allows building relationships over time—all of these things pushed aside by dominant trends, are seen as quaint at best, and usually as irrelevant.

Public work weaves a different reality, a textured tapestry with warp and weft made of the builders' memories, cultural histories, identities, and relationships. In particular, storytelling in the context of public work reveals another element that is key to the pedagogy of public work. To build a future together, we must acknowledge our pasts. In the telling and retelling of individual memories and collective histories, people place the experience of their past in the context of shaping a shared "now." Through narrative, people can deepen their roles as agents and creators of a democratic way of life.

This collection of essays hints at the richness of the narrative imagination and practice involved in public work. It begins to shed light on the democracy we have an opportunity to bring forth today. Pakou Hang in her essay, "A Return to Ban Vinai," tells about her trip "home," only to find that every marker she looked for in Thailand had disappeared. But the going back meant everything to her life here. Eduardo Jurado and Koshin Ahmed reveal how their experiences of public life in Peru and Somalia, respectively, have shaped their passion for democracy in this country. We have learned through many examples in U.S. history that when groups are forced or choose to leave their stories behind to become "American," we all lose.

Recognized or not, everyone who participates at JAS—whether new immigrants, descendants of immigrants or indigenous people—has a narrative shaped by global politics, cultural and family histories, and recent experience. When they emerge, these narratives make an impact on the local place and give texture to the real work people do together. The public process of telling and listening to each other helps people claim a new "we." The typical programmed spaces and technical problem-solving processes people engage in when they defer to professional expertise all too often obscures these resources. Public work does not exclude expert knowledge but it also invites public narrative and encourages a more organic set of interactions, which can tap resources otherwise overlooked.

When JAS participants launched a campaign to raise the visibility of the human-rights abuses of Hmong people in Laotian jungles (the campaign described in Pakou Hang's essay, "Building a Political Consciousness"), people prepared and translated individual and family narratives for inclusion in the briefing book, a fact book presented to legislators, media, and other decision makers. At the capitol press conference, several Hmong people shared their personal narratives publicly, which illuminated the statistical information in powerful ways.

Patricia Hampl, award-winning memoirist, captures the public contribution of such personal narrative:

> There may be no more
> pressing intellectual need in

our culture than for people to become sophisticated about the function of memory. The political implications of the loss of memory are obvious. . . . To write one's life is to tell it twice, and the second living is both spiritual and historical, for a memoir reaches deep within the personality as it seeks its narrative form and it also grasps the life-of-the-times as no political analysis can.[8]

The JAS experience has shown that the craft and public use of narrative are key elements in public work. Narrative gives visibility to individual and collective cultural experience. It highlights cultural traditions and knowledge in a context, that helps others understand similarities and differences. Public work also involves the creation of a collective narrative that JAS tells— the story of people of all ages from diverse places and cultures coming together. In a larger sense, it reminds us all of the story at the heart of American democracy —diverse people can act together in public to improve our common lives—a narrative that more than ever needs to be retold as newcomers find home and as young people grow up to claim their roles as agents and architects of democracy.

Beyond Gated Communities

Authors of these essays struggle for ways to describe the work. Sometimes they say their experience of JAS is "messy" and "chaotic," or unstructured without clear prescription for activity. The challenges of language stem from the fact that public work

Raquel Mendosa gives a fiery speech at the Freedom Festival.

generates a "nonprofessionalized" culture, perhaps better described as organic and flexibly responsive to people who shape it, and also radically against the grain of dominant trends. What many JAS participants first diagnose as an absence of structure—the lack of hierarchy, curriculum, or clearly delineated job descriptions—they later come to see as a *different* structure formed around JAS values. This structure is formed by the values of democratic decision making, through role definitions created in open dialogue and rules generated by participants reflective of the values. When shared values become visible through ongoing dialogue and critical reflection, people learn to use them to re-examine actions and their meanings, a regular exercise important to collective self-governance.

The continual shaping of collective work runs counter to the dominant program-centered and expert-directed ways in which people experience most public spaces today. Programs in the larger culture are created *for* participants; they incorporate pre-determined outcomes and limited roles for participants. Although such programs may have clearer

JAS participants launched a campaign to raise visibility of the human-rights abuses of Hmong people in the Laotian jungles; they are shown in the state capital where they held a well-attended press conference.

expectations and more familiar boundaries, they are also more hierarchical and offer few opportunities for creativity or self-governance. People who work in open-ended spaces like JAS, find wider latitude for

experimentation and cocreation. When prescribed roles and boundaries are suspended, the spaces framed by public work philosophy can be transformative. Sara Carpenter, a long-time participant, expressed it this way:

The annual Freedom Festival, which honors new citizens, people's contributions, and cultures, is part of JAS public work.

[The space] is free—you are allowed to have your opinions and to say what you think. There is no one right answer about an issue. It's acknowledged that issues are very large and complex. There can't be just one answer because here are 15 different people from 15 different places who have 15 different ideas about it. We change the space around to fit our needs as a group. If we need to discuss, then we do that. If we need to bring people in, then we do that. If we need to take a field trip, then that is what we do. We are not boxed in. There is room for exchange. It is not didactic. We share responsibilities with each other. We share information with each other. We have to learn not to be judgmental of each other.

The way for you to have power—and not in the cliché way—is to discover you can get outside the box through learning. It is a political act and hard to do. . . . I came to JAS with my box and said I'm a white woman with a college degree. And they said "Nope, can't sit there." I would hope for people like Alveilo, who is an undocumented immigrant would also not be allowed to stay in that small unhappy box. When he came to JAS, we

said, "Nope, you're a writer and we value the skills that you have. You're no longer just the narrow definition."[9]

Sara's description captures the culture-changing potential that the practice of public work brings to our society. The cultures created in such settings reflect the particularities and local flavor of the participants and their interests. At JAS, we have created rituals like the annual Freedom Festival, regular potluck meals, and cultural exchanges. We've defined different rules of engagement: People both teach and learn; first languages are privileged; people participate rather than observe from the sidelines. We've identified access points that encourage crossing boundaries of culture, language, and age, e.g. paired learning, sharing food, participating in the arts, cross-cultural and cross-generational work and play. As people experience the freedom and power that comes from public work, they take the ideas and practices elsewhere.

Because the emphasis at JAS has been on doing public work rather than on building an organization, a particular kind of "portable" culture has been created. We learned, for example

that to be Hmong does not require that people live in the highlands of China or Laos. People carry their cultural identities with them whether to France, Thailand, Australia, or Minnesota. Likewise, many JAS participants develop a particular identity with a strong democratic sensibility. Terri Wilson's reflections in "A Call to Vocation" on the lasting impact of her experience working in such a democratic space typifies what we hear from many JAS participants who have moved on. Thus when people carry democratic values, attitudes, and practices with them, the culture tends to spread to other spaces.

In the context of today's turbulent world, most people feel overwhelmed and powerless. As a result, they retreat into smaller and smaller circles of private life where they do have some control, even as they suspect that retreat spells trouble. "If you look at the whole picture of everything that is wrong, it is so overwhelming," said one woman from Richmond in a focus group sponsored by the Kettering Foundation. "You just retreat back and take care of what you know you can take care of— and you make it smaller, make it even down to just you and your unit. You know you can take care of that."[10]

JAS counters such retreat into gated communities of the mind as well as living environments. It has been a seedbed of theory and practice for wider democratic culture change, whose lessons, we believe, have wide application. Perhaps its most important product is simply, realistic hope. Hope grows from the experiences of change within ourselves and within our immediate environments. A language of hope emerges from the richness of the ideas germinating at JAS, a language that we can bring to the public work of changing the world.

---

[1] Harry Boyte founded Project Public Life in 1989 at the Humphrey Institute of Public Affairs. PPL focused on developing practical theory from on-the-ground efforts to renew public life in low-income and blue-collar communities, in professionalized service institutions where expert-client patterns had replaced productive public interactions, and in communities, which require for their civic renewal new patterns of fluid, open interactions among their institutions and residents. Many partners in a variety of settings have contributed to this theory-building work.

[2] Harry Boyte and Nan Kari, *Building America: The Democratic Promise of Public Work* (Philadelphia, PA: Temple Press, 1996).

[3] Harry Boyte argued in his article "Off the Playground of Civil Society," *A PEGS Journal: The Good Society* (Winter 1999-2000), that the dominant political map that locates citizenship in the realm of civil society separated from business and government and that defines the citizen as paradigmatically a volunteer marginalizes and domesticates citizenship while making it impossible to address with democratic power many of the challenges of the world today. See also Boyte, *Everyday Politics: Reconnecting Citizens and Public Life* (2004) for elaborations of these arguments.

[4] It is important to note that the increase in the immigrant population in Minnesota in 2000 is only about 5 percent of the population compared with a much more dramatic rise in 1900 when the number of new immigrants was 30 percent of the total population. In 1900, two-thirds came from Germany, Sweden, and Norway. In 2000, the breakdown was different: 17 percent from Europe, 40 percent from Asia, 24 percent from Latin America, and 13 percent from Africa. (Source: *Immigration in Minnesota: Discovering Common Ground*, Minneapolis Foundation Publication, 2005, p. 3.)

[5] The Saint Paul Public School district is the largest in the state. In 2005, the Saint Paul schools' 41,000 students spoke 97 different languages. Seventy-two percent are students of color; sixty-nine percent receive free or reduced-price lunches; thirty-seven percent are learning English as a second language. In the early 1980s, the district had about 3,500 students from immigrant families; today there are over 16,000—including 1,200 new Hmong students recently arrived. (Source: Minneapolis Foundation, 2005.)

[6] Reggio Emilia, is a city in Northern Italy, where over the past 40 years, educators and parents have developed a body of pedagogical thought and practices through early childhood centers. In this democratic philosophy, teachers, children, and parents are all central to the learning project, which itself is the subject of continual study. Reggio-inspired educators assert that learning is an ongoing process of constructing, testing, and reconstructing theories. In 2004, Reggio's traveling exhibit, The Hundred Languages of Children, was displayed in the basement of the St. Paul City Hall, where many from the West Side NLC and JAS had an opportunity to view it. Inspired by the approach to democratic education and its embrace of place, West Side parents and other NLC leaders, formed a partnership with the Minnesota Children's Museum and a group of Reggio-inspired educators to help develop a series of workshops for community leaders to introduce the pedagogy and process of documentation. At the end of summer 2005, the Minnesota Children's Museum presented an exhibit, Creating a Culture of Learning on the West Side, which helped make children's learning in the summer program visible and public.

[7] Sara Carpenter, interviewed by Nan Kari, October 2001.

[8] Patricia Hampl, *I Could Tell You Stories* (New York, NY: W. W. Norton & Company, 1999), 36-37.

[9] Sara Carpenter interview.

[10] Richard C. Harwood, "The Nation's Looking Glass," *Kettering Review* (Spring 2000): 15-16, 17-18.

Part Two:
PLACE MATTERS

Part Two:
PLACE MATTERS

Reinvigoration of a democratic culture requires a recovery of what was once called the commons—public spaces, open to all and generative in their diversity. Public space invites connections among people. These public relationships form the heart of a working democracy. Reopening these spaces, however, is no easy task. Many of us have forgotten what they look like or how to use them. If we are to renew democracy and to understand ourselves as public actors, we will need to struggle with this challenge.

The work can't be done in cyberspace—although the Internet has unique capacity to build organizing networks. Rather, it requires face-to-face relationship building in real places. The absence of a sense of grounding in a real community for so many people in our society is an acute loss, not only for immigrants trying to make a new home, but also for native-born citizens and the larger society. Public spaces owned and used by people in local communities, especially places

that commingle immigrants' histories and cultures with the traditions of native-born Americans can be an extraordinary contribution to the revitalization of civic life and democracy. At JAS, we have seen this firsthand.

We have found that most people have a deep yearning to know their roots, the place from which they were transplanted. Discovering ways to belong in a new place while honoring and recognizing the importance of one's origin is a pressing and

sometimes unrecognized task for new immigrants. Dominant messages that call for assimilation of new arrivals deny the validity of such work. Interestingly, many college students, who have grown up in the United States, have little knowledge of their own family stories and also suffer from an absence of connection to specific geographic communities and family narratives. Pakou Hang writes about her return to Ban Vinai only to find corn and rice fields where familiar buildings used to stand. In some ways her story reflects what is happening in many of our neighborhoods and small towns here. Where are the markers that help us remember and keep us grounded? How can we reengage in relational and rich cultural traditions, in a society that so highly prizes mobility in search of success? If we are to reclaim civic life, our identities need roots in particular places. In a profound way, this challenges the arrogant, uprooted version of "the American Dream."

In the twenty-first century, the idea of public life is a contested one. Tensions arise as policymakers seek the correct balance between private and public ownership and responsibilities. In the current climate, the private side is often better resourced—"people should pay for what they want and need for themselves." Yet the public side—the commons—depends on a rapidly decreasing tax base and shared values that contribute to the betterment of all. In many ways this reflects the ubiquitous tension between individual and community, always a feature of American life. But it takes on new forms in our frenet-

ic, consumer-oriented, intensely competitive society. As we have increasingly lost our identities as productive citizens, and as consumer lifestyles have come to define the American dream, the very idea of community often becomes defined by lifestyle choices based on shopping patterns or Internet chat rooms. In this context, reemphasizing the critical importance of place and the practices and cultures that grow up around places becomes a vital strategy in strengthening civic life.

Place matters because civic identity is rooted in a particular place and expresses the public side of that place. A particular place that we call home or neighborhood or community is complex and manifests itself in a variety of rich patterns. These places give people the opportunity to listen to the voices and the memories of those who live and work there, and then together they can build a history. Anonymity, silence, and isolation give way. This has been the experience at JAS.

The examples of space and place as described in these essays are both physical and conceptual.

Nan Skelton's "Framing Democratic Space" contrasts the limitations of institutional public space with the kind of free and generative space that JAS seeks to create, where people can experience power, exercise creativity, and practice democracy. "A Sense of Place" by D'Ann Urbaniak Lesch invites us into a JAS circle space and brings its occupants—immigrants, college students, and educators—to life for one brief evening. In "The Borderland," Derek Johnson tells the story of his two weddings with Rebecca Ryan—one, a Western-style ceremony, and the other conducted at JAS in the Somali tradition. As Johnson puts it, "We became engaged in a marriage of ideas and customs and hopes. Together, we formed a more perfect union." Finally, Pakou Hang, in her essay "Return to Ban Vinai," tells about her trip "home" to Thailand only to find that the place where she had been born was no longer home. "There is a seduction attached to the notion of place," she writes. But roots can be transplanted, she discovered, and the place she calls home, has shifted now, as has her identity.

FRAMING DEMOCRATIC SPACE

by Nan Skelton

Democracy needs living public spaces, but today's world tends to extinguish them. The Jane Addams School for Democracy offers lessons for the creation and growth of democratic space, against the grain of a society that is focused on individual achievement, expert domination, and efficiency.

Setting the Stage

The Jane Addams School relocated "up the hill" to Humboldt Senior High School in January 2002 in order to accommodate an increasing number of families and college students. Our affiliation with the St. Paul Public School district (SPPS) through a partnership with community education made the transition a smooth one. The physical qualities of the high-school space and patterns of interaction that typically occur there, however, came into high relief as JAS settled in. We regularly struggle with the limitations of the public-school environment as we

try to maintain the fluid, open patterns of interaction that characterize JAS. This contrast highlights the concept of democratic space in important ways.

The neighborhood high school was built in the 1960s as a replacement for an older building. The new school was the result of a citizen initiative led by young Latino activists demanding a new educational facility in their low-income immigrant community. Their march across the river to the state capital marks one of the signal moments of Minnesota "Latino power" in the 1960s. The building of Humboldt High

School remains a proud chapter in West Side history.

Today the interior walls recall another era with their 1970s red and orange. Shiny, tiled floors and institutional design reflect the generic, sterile educational culture that has taken hold in much of American public education. Security guards sit like gatekeepers at the only open door in the front of the building. Handwritten notes are tacked up on posts and boards and remain long after their messages cease to be relevant. The lack of visually interesting classrooms suggests a design focused more on management than everyday human interaction. Very little in the environment reflects the individuality of teachers, students, or perhaps most telling of all, the neighborhood in which the school resides.

Even though Humboldt Senior High School is a public building, there are few indications that the public (as in the people) controls this space. The dominant message conveys: *the space belongs to the school district*. For many public schools, their uses and rules are determined by people largely invisible to the public, communicated through arcane policies, and enforced by custodians constantly anxious about scratches on waxed floors. Consequently, people have almost forgotten that schools are an important public resource. The lack of aesthetic qualities reflects a pattern that has become commonplace in American public education: disconnection of public schools from the life of the community. The idea of public space understood in its fullest sense remains only a distant institutional memory. Instead, public schools have embraced practices that mimic the privatized culture with the unfortunate result that most people take for granted that public schools do not really belong to the public.[1]

Yet the 1971 Minnesota Community Education Statute reminds us of what was once the more public nature of public-school buildings:

> The purpose of sections 124D.18 and 124D.19 is to make maximum use of the public schools of Minnesota by the community and to expand utilization by the school of the human resources of the community, by establishing a community education program.

What messages would students and teachers hear if schools were places of beauty, community connection, and human sociability? What does space have to do with creating a public culture? Everything!

Humboldt High School, St. Paul, Minnesota

Alternative Spaces

Two strands of thinking about the physical qualities of public spaces and the cultural dimensions of such spaces help clarify the complex idea of democratic space, which implies an interplay between physical setting, social expectation, and patterns of behavior.

Project for Public Spaces (PPS), a resource in New York that works with citizens on "placemaking" in markets, parks, neighborhoods, and other public environments, offers a useful framework. "Start with the Petunias," says Fred Kent, PPS president. He means that revitalization of places begins with small steps. How people use the space ought to direct the physical design rather than the other way around. Intentional use of spaces can transform them into lively public environments.

His advice parallels what we do at the high school. Simple things have opened the door to reconceptualization of the space. Regular potluck celebrations where people share each other's cultural foods transform the institutional feel of the school cafeteria. A display of a large handmade, group-designed quilt

An ofrenda *celebrating the Day of the Dead in the hallway at Humboldt High School*

depicting freedom narratives reminds participants that the space belongs to them. In classrooms, immigrants hold public conversations with legislators, school-board members, and park directors. When people claim and shape spaces as their own, they experience them in powerful ways.

Fred Kent, who has spent years helping communities reclaim their public spaces, notes that seeing people engaged in the activities and life of great public spaces is to see them at their best.

> [People] come out of themselves; they participate in community life; they learn

the mores of their culture and community. Good spaces breed good activity. Bad spaces breed little to no positive activity and are often a breeding ground for negative activity.[2]

Sara Evans and Harry Boyte pursue another line of thinking about space in their analysis of the well-springs of democratic movements. They write:

> Free spaces are settings between private lives and large-scale institutions where ordinary citizens can act with dignity, independence, and vision. These are forms of association with a relatively open and participatory character, grounded in the fabric of community life.[3]

When people create free spaces, they generate cultural alternatives to dominant patterns of hierarchy, control, and generic, impersonal systems and institutional culture. Free spaces serve as "schools for democracy," where people build public as well as private relationships and transform themselves from victims to actors. In these settings, people can claim the role of citizen in its richest sense.

JAS aims to create a free space inside the high school—a place where people can experience power and exercise creativity. Our assumption at JAS was, that if people feel they are an active part of what happens at Humboldt, they would claim the place as their own.

When public schools shut themselves off from the public, we intuitively recognize it as a violation of something essential to a democratic society. But such walling off can be reversed. The simple and ordinary common ways we have of coming together as people in the Jane Addams School make it possible for us to bring democratic life to this public place. The events that happen there—reading, playing, the rush of children, the potlucks, the celebrations of Eid, Day of the Dead, and the Posada, the candidate forums, cooking together, sharing stories of home, loss, and becoming citizens, and laughing together over language struggles—these are the diverse activities that make this commons come to life. Christopher Alexander, contemporary architect and theorist known for his design of a human-scale architectural system called a patterned language, writes:

> Those of us who are concerned with buildings tend to forget too easily that all the life and soul of a place, all of our experiences there, depend not simply on the physical environment, but on the patterns of events, which we experience there.[4]

If we can come together on a common ground, we can reestablish our communities as the foundation of a democratic society. The JAS community-building agenda aspires to reconnect the school with the community and to catalyze culture change in the neighborhood and public-school system, while schooling all of us in the skills, habits, and attitudes of democratic citizenship.

One key lesson from the JAS experience is that citizens and neighborhood residents are willing to take leadership in reclaiming public spaces, because they add quality to neighborhood life and invite new relationships among neighbors. West Siders have repeatedly demonstrated the spirit, ingenuity, will, and persistence needed to create an alternative to the technocratic cultures often assumed to be a given. The public work of creating such spaces suggests practical and conceptual lessons for broader democratic change and renewal in the society.

Nicole Ly shows a story cloth that chronicles the journey of Hmong immigrants from Laos to the United States. Near the bottom of the tapestry, many of them can be seen crossing the Mekong River.

ahead. . . . The work was creative; it was like making a poem, or dancing, or saying a prayer.[5]

Our rural memories shaped the metaphors we used as we labored to keep the space open for experimentation, to embrace the reality that JAS was a work in progress, to recognize that we would not always succeed and simply, to "let the dough rise."

And we remembered the storytelling, the music, and the market squares that were important in our villages in Laos, Mexico, and El Salvador. Telling the stories that were told in the villages in Laos, again in this new place, helped us understand that, in order to create a place that was inclusive and generative, we would need to keep telling these stories and make new ones. The market square also served as a visual reminder that we could not develop a public life without attending to our physical place. Daniel Kemmis, contemporary writer, thinker, and politician, addresses the relationship between space and public life. As he sees it:

> The demise of public life has to be understood in terms of space (or place) as well as time. . . . Public life can only be reclaimed by understanding, and then practicing its connection to real, identifiable places. . . . (Political) culture may be shaped by its place, as well as by its (historical) time.[6]

We *reflected*. Because we were squatters in a public school relying on what our listening and memories were teaching us, we understood that shared group reflections needed to be a critical part of our process. We found all too often that there were very few existing public spaces to serve as examples. In order to teach ourselves, we interrogated everything we did. When we became sloppy and put reflection aside, we paid the price by drifting off course. Over time this practice has improved. Being surrounded by the nondemocratic environments of public schools and bureaucratically heavy institutions, such as the University of Minnesota and the Bureau of Citizenship and Immigration Services, has generated insights.

Using these processes of listening, remembering, and reflecting, we gradually began to build a place where we could express democratic values and practices. On the one hand, it was a microeffort, a seedbed for our own learning. On the other, our work can reveal to larger worlds what it takes to understand that, as Wendell Berry puts it, "We and our country create one another."[7]

Democracy's Roots

From another vantage point, a lesson that is crucial but also difficult because it goes so much against the grain of our efficiency-minded, fast-paced society is that the work of democracy takes time. The philosopher-architect, Christopher Alexander reminds us:

> Possibly the most basic and necessary feature of any living process is that it goes gradually. We cannot create unfolded living structure by drawing it, as if it had unfolded and then building it by different means. It really must unfold in real time.[8]

Place matters because people live there over extended time; they form relationships there; they make concrete and tactical sense of the world there. A place is where people feel rooted and connected. The danger is that in our highly mobile lives we will settle for those anonymous *in betweens* where roots cannot form.

When we began JAS, we wanted to ground it, with fluid and permeable boundaries in a place, a specific neighborhood, in ways that would draw from community life and contribute to that life as well. The West Side became that place; its history and residents have shaped those who live there now. As a group of people, we also contribute to the revitalization of a neighborhood culture from the inside out. The work of JAS is relationship centered and citizen oriented. It helps to shape the culture of the community.

A complicated set of dynamics works against a strong sense of place in neighborhoods today. Many community-located institutions have the rhetoric of place, but in reality focus inside their own walls. City and statewide systems that impact neighborhoods make decisions at levels far beyond the reach and influence

of citizens. Many urban neighborhoods experience constant flux, with groups moving in and out as economic situations change. People in neighborhoods attend different schools, churches, and work elsewhere. This dislocation impacts everyone and the community as a whole. JAS aims to counter these phenomena by grounding people in the history of the place and building relationships that connect participants with other organizations and residents. Engaging in public work creates the space and the space we inhabit comes alive.

Democracy's Structures

Another sharp contrast with professional cultures in schools and elsewhere—routinized, standardized, based on predictable outcomes and controllable behaviors—is the structural nature of the Jane Addams School. Early on, we developed and maintained a fairly simple structure that gave all of us a framework within which to learn, develop, experiment, improvise, and create. The simplicity of the structure meant that all of us—children, college students, new immigrants, people speaking a variety of languages, faculty members—could both maintain and access the space. The specific encoded rules of the structure included:

- Everyone is free to raise issues or develop ideas for discussion at weekly meetings held prior to the evening session.

- College students convene twice a week for orientation and reflection.

- People meet in learning circles organized by language.

- Weekly gatherings begin with group conversation followed by work with learning partners.

- All group discussions and public forums are translated into the languages of the group members. Anyone who is bilingual may be asked to translate.

- The Children's Circle includes a reading and discussion time followed by group projects initiated, created, and led by the children with their college-student partners.

Within this structure those who show up make the decisions about what will be learned, who

will teach, how the activities will be designed, and what materials will be used. The rules governing the space have evolved over time in a slow process of accretion to which many people have contributed. They are simple enough that everyone can monitor and maintain them. Within this structure, most people find ways to

contribute ideas, talents, and effort. We continually struggle to keep the space open and free for everyone who participates. Too much control reduces the possibilities for creativity and new learning. With too little structure or unclear purposes, people experience chaos. Finding and main-

taining that balance challenges everyone. When it works well, the public space provides a place to experience public life and engage in a political culture.

In 2004, I learned of the growth, creation, and struggles within the Internet world and about Open Source Software (OSS), which means that people can read, adapt, improve, fix bugs, and redistribute software with amazing speed. Oddly, I found in the Internet/OSS story familiar patterns of improvisation, exploration, and fluidity across borders that parallel the JAS story.

In the 1970s, Richard Stallman, while at Harvard, began working at A-l Lab with a group of exceptional programmers, exploring and inventing the worlds of computing.

Although there was no real plan to his work—"I was just going along doing my usual think-up-a-feature-and-add-it type stuff," Stallman says—the result was one of the most famous and powerful pieces of software ever written . . . the editor program called Emacs.[9]

Eventually Stallman and his group figured out how to run Emacs on new hardware so it could spread throughout the World Wide Web. Stallman established an informal rule that anyone could make improvements to the program provided they shared it with everyone. The ideas of open access and sharing were central to maintaining innovation and democratization of the Internet.

Stallman and his colleagues worked hard to build it and to ensure that it remained outside the exclusive control of government or a private individual. They fought against the imposition of rules or copyright protections. "Built on a platform that is controlled, the protocols of the Internet have erected a free space of innovation. These . . . networks have created an open resource that any can draw upon and that many have."[10] Writing on this subject Lawrence Lessig, Professor of Law at Stanford Law School and founder of the school's Center for Internet and Society, suggests:

> The Internet has provided for much of the world the greatest demonstration of the power of freedom. . . . My central claim throughout is

that there is a benefit to resources held in common and that the Internet is the best evidence of that benefit. . . . Yet so blind are we to the possible value of a commons that we don't even notice the commons that the Internet is. And, in turn, this blindness leads us to ignore changes to the norms and architecture of the Net that weaken this commons.[11]

Peter Levine, associate director of the Center for Information and Research on Civic Learning and Engagement (CIRCLE), has observed the multiple public work qualities involved in the creation of Internet technology. The Internet was the product of an enormously diverse set of actors, working in many contexts—government, academia, business, research centers, and backyard laboratories, and it aimed at creation of a commons that would be open to all.[12]

This effort to recover a commons both on the Internet and in physical public spaces is at the heart of reviving our democracy. It is difficult to do. There is no set blueprint. The process has to reflect the context and people who generate it. JAS experiences illustrate in multiple ways both the possibilities and the challenges of creating the spaces and places for democracy to take root.

[1] Daniel Kemmis, *Community and the Politics of Place* (Norman, OK: University of Oklahoma Press, 1990). Kemmis explains, "A people so constituted is, in turn, the only genuine source of meaning for the word *public*, which in Latin meant 'of the people.' It does not simply mean 'of people.' People in their separated individuality never become public." See page 4.

[2] Fred Kent, *"What Is a Great Civic Space?"* Project for Public Spaces Web site, www.PPS.org.

[3] Sara Evans and Harry Boyte, *Free Spaces* (Chicago, IL: University of Chicago Press, 1992), 17-18.

[4] Christopher Alexander, *A Timeless Way of Building* (New York, NY: Oxford University Press), 62.

[5] Paul Gruchow, *Grass Roots: The Universe of Home* (Minneapolis, MN: Milkweed Editions, 1995), 19-20.

[6] Daniel Kemmis, *Community and the Politics of Place* (Norman, OK: University of Oklahoma Press, 1990), 6.

[7] Wendell Berry, *The Unsettling of America* (New York, NY: Avon Books, 1977), 22.

[8] Christopher Alexander, *The Nature of Order: An Essay on the Art of Building and the Nature of the Universe*, Book Two (Berkeley, CA: Center for Environmental Structure, 2002-2004), 230-231.

[9] Glyn Moody, *Rebel Code, Linux and the Open Source Revolution* (New York, NY: Basic Books, 2001), 16.

[10] Lawrence Lessig, *The Future of Ideas* (New York, NY: Vintage Books, 2001), 26.

[11] Ibid., 15, 23.

[12] Peter Levine, "Can the Internet Rescue Democracy?" in *Democracy's Moment: Reforming the American Political System for the 21st Century*, eds. Ronald Hayduk and Kevin Mattson (Lanham, MD: Rowman & Littlefield, 2002), 121-137.

THE BORDERLAND

by Derek Johnson

Anticipation was already running high as members of the JAS East African Circle gathered in June 2005, at Humboldt High. Although it was unusually warm for the first day of summer in Minnesota, the weather was the last thing on anyone's mind as they carried armload after armload of food into the school's cafeteria, resulting in an aromatic array of specialties from Somalia, Ethiopia, and other East African countries.

Talking and laughing, they arranged each brimming platter and bowl on a line of tables stretching 50 feet across the room.

The men and women had been preparing all week to host the festivities about to take place: a mock Somali wedding for me and my wife, Rebecca Ryan. Both of us had worked for some time at JAS, I as the coordinator of the East African Circle, and Rebecca as a member of that circle, where most of us thought of ourselves not only as fellow learners and teachers, but as friends. Everyone at JAS shared in our joy when we became engaged, and many members of the circle were guests

at our wedding that May on St. Paul's Harriet Island along the Mississippi River. Most of them had not attended a Western-style wedding before, and Rebecca and I were delighted when they asked to reciprocate by holding a Somali-style marriage ceremony for us.

"All of JAS should come as our guests," urged Koshin Ahmed, the circle's Somali facilitator. He and other members assured everyone that this special occasion would be a welcome opportunity for mutual discovery, offered in the JAS spirit of reciprocal learning. We who were non-Muslims could witness and learn about

Muslim ceremonies; Somalis could share these ceremonies with those outside their religion. In some respects, our Somali "marriage" was to become a metaphor for what JAS does: it opens a kind of borderland space in which people form relationships by experiencing each other's cultures in unique ways.

Through the leadership of six to eight Somalis from the East African Circle, the group worked together to plan the details of the celebration, making sure that everyone played a contributing role. Koshin would be the cultural translator. Everyone would contribute traditional foods for the reception. The women from the planning group would dress and adorn the bride. All Rebecca and I needed to do was to attend and enjoy ourselves.

The night before the celebration, the women met with Rebecca and decorated her hands and arms with henna in traditional wedding designs. They presented her with jewelry and a traditional wedding dress, which Asli had made. After doing the final fitting, they explained to Rebecca what she could expect during the ceremony. I, on the other hand, had been told nothing other than to wear the dress shirt and pants I wore at our wedding in May. The elders would give me the rest of my instructions at the ceremony.

By half past seven the night of June 21, about 200 people milled about in the high-school cafeteria, 75 of them past and present participants of the East African Circle. Standing at the front of the room, I took in the colorful tableau: Somali women dressed in beautiful flowing dresses and *hijabs*, some of which covered all but their eyes, others covering just their hair. Men in rimless, flat-topped hats that stood about an inch high on their

Rebecca Ryan and Derek Johnson, the bride and groom

heads. Children dressed in their finest formal clothing to signify the important occasion. Hmong, Latino, and native-born American adults and children, including many college students, all dressed in western clothes. To the casual observer, the scene looked hodge-podge, disconnected in its lack

of uniformity. To me, it felt harmonious, united by our desire to share and learn from our differences.

All of us were waiting for directions about the roles we would play—not to mention waiting for the bride to appear. The ceremony was to begin at 7:30

that evening, but it took Rebecca's attendants longer than expected to dress her. Heads turned as she finally entered the room, draped in a diaphanous gown, flame-red and shimmering with threads of gold. Her arms and fingers were adorned with gold bracelets and rings. The women who assisted Rebecca beamed with pride as they saw the crowd's happy reaction to the beautiful bride.

At last, everyone was formally welcomed to the celebration. In Somali and English, we were told that the wedding would represent only the briefest highlights of a traditional Somali wedding, which typically lasts five or six days. Then the guests were divided into two groups: women seated on one side, men on the other. I stood beside the Somali male elders in front of the guests, my curiosity rising at what was to take place. Rebecca stayed near the back of the room, almost out of sight, hidden behind a circle of Somali women.

The celebration began with a negotiation for dowry and a formal acceptance of the marriage. The oldest East African man acted as the lead negotiator. Two men chosen by the elders each represented the bride's family and the groom. The representative for Rebecca requested a horse from my representative, who consented to the request. The ceremony itself consisted of readings in English and Somali from the Qur'an, led by a Somali elder dressed in a flowing knee-length shirt. We didn't catch every

nuance, of course, but the context in which the words were spoken was clear. For all of us, the engagement in the moment was wholehearted, involving not just our intellect but our senses and emotions. We were experiencing and learning and knowing at every level.

After the ceremony, the elder wished Rebecca and me much happiness and invited everyone to feast. The two of us took our honored place at the front of the long lines snaking through the cafeteria. We felt nourished by the food as well as the friendship. As instructed, we circulated among the guests as they dined and thanked them for attending. Traditional strains of Somali music began to blare from a boombox as people finished their meals. Soon, dancers gathered in a great Somali circle of celebration, joined by Hmong and Latino adults and children as well as several college students. The sense of community, the excitement of codiscovery that emanated from that circle was the culmination of all of our anticipation and hopes for that night's event.

In the borderland we created that night—the shared space in which our opportunities for personal and cultural communication were limitless—we reached out to one another in mutual trust and respect. In teaching and learning from each other, we created and nurtured our sense of community. We became engaged in a marriage of ideas and customs and hopes. Together, we formed a more perfect union.

A SENSE OF PLACE

by D'Ann Urbaniak Lesch

A community is a multilayered and densely textured organism. In events remembered, challenges overcome, and the passage of time itself, its characters find their place and the understanding of their purpose.

Kathleen Hirsch, *A Home in the Heart of a City*

It is seven o'clock on a Wednesday evening in August 1999, and 37 people are crammed into a hot room, doors propped open for air. All of us—immigrant families, college students, neighbors—are here to *participate* in the Hmong adult circle of the Jane Addams School for Democracy.

Some are here to study citizenship, to work on their English, to learn with people of different backgrounds. Some seek a place in which to belong, to share, to laugh, and to cry. Others want a place to learn and teach traditions and skills important to them. We begin the session as we always do, with a 30-minute cultural exchange. The conversation I lead tonight as a JAS organizer moves in many directions: New members tell why they have come to JAS;

Vue volunteers to lead a discussion on upcoming political campaigns; Catherine offers to help Vue since she is already working on two of the campaigns; Shao talks about which Hmong foods she will make for us tonight.

The half hour passes quickly, and as people regroup in learning pairs, there is a buzz about the room that spills into the hallway, side rooms, and even the kitchen where Shao is working. Martha and Mai Lor, a new citizen, look

at a book on Alaska, where Mai Lor's husband wants to go on vacation with their family of nine. Erik teaches basic English to Chong, a woman of 60 or so who repeats the words, smiles, and points to their matching pictures. Nan and Plua huddle close, talking about Plua's children, family life, and the driver's test she wants to take. Dave works with Ying and Toua, both of whom failed the citizenship test and are trying with great fervor to

Mai Lor (right) teaches a cooking class.

learn everything all over again. Meanwhile, Shao cooks squash and sticky rice, piling them on plates for all of us to share. That so much can go on at once is the beauty of our work.

All of us have been coming to JAS for some time. Getting along is a big part of our diverse community. We developed trust and recognized that, whoever we are, each of us is important. We

believe that if you have something to share—cooking, farming, sewing, storytelling, music, humor—you have something to contribute. We have discovered that we have much to learn from one another. In fact, several communities exist within JAS because we have created several learning circles. The circles themselves, many of whose members are committed to showing up every

Monday and Wednesday evening, have a rich sense of place and belonging.

The reality is that creating a sense of place takes time. New people coming to JAS may need weeks or months before they comfortably participate. The right opportunity must present itself at the right moment, sometimes more than once, before a person risks getting involved. That is why the continuity of the space is so important. A community depends on stability, but it must also embrace change. Whoever shows up helps determine what we do and who we are as a group. As people come and go and as new voices merge with old, the space itself persists. When the open, fluid quality of the circle space works well, it fosters learning, helps people build confidence, strengthens relationships, and contributes to the JAS community as a whole.

The routines and expectations help to develop a sense of community, especially when there is so much fluidity. In the adult learning circles, for instance, the back-and-forth, give-and-take bilingual cultural exchanges occur as if by second nature, as if this is how conversation happens everywhere. The method conveys the value JAS places on everyone's understanding and participation. We refuse to create a space where every culture is valued and then, by our actions, treat people as though their native language is their disability. Even something as simple as placing chairs in a circle helps reinforce a sense of community. Any initial discomfort in sitting next to someone "different"

becomes something less than that—and something more—as people discover how to build relationships across differences typically seen as barriers.

We have found that to break through barriers, we must be ready for the different ways in which people overcome them. For years, JAS has been a safe environment for such individuals. Here, immigrant women who have been limited by their gender roles to domestic and parenting work try new roles that allow them to lead, teach, and translate,

either one-on-one or in groups, and to inspire other women like themselves. Immigrant families who have lacked access and opportunity to participate in public activities travel with the school to games, museums, concerts, and the state capital, interacting with fellow sports fans, enjoying art and music, and engaging in political debate. Children and elders who have been dismissed for being too young or too old, teach and learn from each other and everyone in between, whether they're conquering the alphabet

D'Ann Urbaniak Lesch

or a citizenship test. Immigrant men and women, finding their voices in public, voice speak through translators, and bilingual young people, once embarrassed to speak in their native languages, are encouraged to help members of dual cultures see the other's point of view.

At JAS, we believe in the abilities of each individual, and we also realize that people working together can create change. Living out democratic ideals requires community connections. When participants divide into learning pairs or small groups, they form connections apart from the larger circle or the whole of JAS. If the partners work together over time, then their learning is strengthened by the trust and comfort and security that develop between them. We take seriously the words of one participant who said, "To feel safe is not something that can be easily created. We trust each other because we have built a relationship."

The diversity that plays an important role in the success of our community also plays an important role in my outlook on life. I feel and understand things I would never have experienced or understood except through the people who gather here. JAS gives us all a place to see life through the eyes of another. That became especially clear to me one Wednesday night at JAS, when I invited Chong to share with the group her story of passing her citizenship test. Even though her immigration papers place her age at around 45, Chong is closer to 60—either that, or she has aged tremendously since coming to America, having left her home in Laos and, later, the Thai refugee camp that she was forced to call home. I had come to know Chong by making sure she got to JAS on Hmong Circle nights and helping her prepare for her test.

Chong Chang (right) at her swearing-in ceremony, with D'Ann Urbaniak Lesch and the judge

Taking turns with an English translator, Chong described to the group what the test administrator had asked her and how she had answered. When the examiner asked whether or not she would change her name, Chong replied, "No I am too old and used to it." She explained that since it had not been snowy or rainy that day, the good weather made it possible for her to pass the test. All the Hmong people laughed at this; later, when I heard the translated version of her talk, I realized how sometimes much is missed between language and culture, that between the words lies meaning that some can see and feel and others can't, no matter how good the translation.

Chong's story was greeted by cheers from everyone in the room, and I smiled to see her clapping humbly for herself along with members of the circle. She sat down in her chair and I got up from mine, prepared to move on to the next topic. But within seconds, Chong returned to the front of the room with something in her hand.

"This is the story cloth I made about my experience at Jane Addams School," she said, holding up a small white piece of fabric,

vibrant images leaping from the clean, bright material. "This is Plua up here in the corner. She knew I was lonely at home so she told me to come to JAS. Even though I didn't think I would be able to learn, I came with her. This is me at the bottom. . . . Right here (pointing at the top right), this is Judy. Judy worked with me often, looking at pictures with me, teaching me words. Next to me is D'Ann. She picked me up every night. She must love me more than my own family. She made sure I got to the test and helped me. This, off to the side, is the lawyer who helped me qualify for the Hmong Veterans Bill because I am a widow of a soldier. And this (pointing to the middle) is Xiong (Mitch, a graduate student fluent in Hmong), who worked with me and sometimes drove me home. Pang (pointing to the bottom right) helped me study the questions in Hmong and took me to the test. Below everyone's image are their names written in Hmong. And at the very bottom I wrote: 2002 1 29. That is the date I passed my test.

"I want D'Ann to have this story cloth."

"She must love me more than

my own family." What had I done to deserve such praise? Had I treated Chong with the same care and understanding she treated me while sewing my name into her fabric? Had I worked to see things through her eyes—the eyes of an aging Hmong woman who traveled across the ocean to a land she didn't understand and that didn't understand her? As my eyes began to fill with tears, Chong presented me with another gift: a beautiful Hmong coat for my daughter. Chong had never met my daughter, yet with the coat she acknowledged my child as part of an even larger community, one that now welcomed her as a citizen.

Sewn as characters within the greater story of our richly textured community at JAS are the learners who want to be there and want to be a part of something important together. In listening to and learning from each other, we can transcend political, ethnic, and language divides that might otherwise exist. In overcoming challenges together, we have realized what we can accomplish. In understanding our purpose, we have found our sense of place.

These are the ties that bind.

RETURN TO BAN VINAI

by Pakou Hang

always imagined that when I would return to the place I was born, my body and my soul would automatically recognize it. The picture, the smell, the sound of the place would be embedded in my cellular and spiritual memory, just waiting to be reactivated.

I was born in 1976 in a Thai refugee camp called Ban Vinai. When I was in college, I saw pictures of it for the first time. An American anthropologist had written a children's book about Ban Vinai, and as I licked my fingers and turned the glossy pages, I remember seeing brown grass huts and brown dirt floors, brown trucks with brown bottles in the trunk, brown children staring back at me in brown torn clothes with skinny brown legs. I remember wondering if I would see pictures of my older sister and cousins, who had played in the camp's soccer field and along its dirt roads.

My parents grew up in Laos where my father served as a captain in the Hmong secret army. They were allied with the United States during the Vietnam War. After the war, when the communists took over Laos, my father surely would have been arrested and imprisoned, if not for my uncle, who riding a bus home from boarding school saw military tanks rolling towards our village. He jumped off the bus, and quickly ran home to alert my father. That night, my mother, my father, and my older sister secretly fled our village, made their way across the Mekong River into Thailand, then arrived in Ban Vinai.

My parents lived in Ban Vinai for a couple of months. My father helped build a school and cleared a soccer field where children could play. Fifteen days after I was born my parents, my older sister, and I boarded an airplane to Atlanta, Georgia, in the United States. My parents did not speak English and no one they met there spoke Hmong. We lived in Georgia for two lonely months before my parents decided to move to Providence, Rhode Island, to reunite with my maternal grandparents. In 1979, my younger brother was born. He was diagnosed with a rare kidney disease and the doctors stressed that one of his kidneys had to be removed. My parents were frantic. Hmong culture prohibits the extraction of internal organs, in the belief that if the body is not whole at the time of death, the spirit will roam endlessly searching for all its parts. And so, fearful of reprisal, my family fled Rhode Island to Appleton, Wisconsin, where I grew up. I attended Catholic school there, joined the local Brownie troop, rode my bike around the neighborhood, and even started a girls-only club with my Hmong and white friends in the third grade. My brother with the alleged kidney problem (which never materialized), used to follow me to our secret clubhouse, but we wouldn't let him join. I loved Appleton. It is the place of my happiest childhood memories.

In 1987, my family moved to St. Paul, Minnesota, to open a Chinese restaurant business. There were seven children in the family now. The restaurant flopped, but we stayed in Minnesota and in 1995, I graduated from Mounds Park Academy in St. Paul. Shortly after graduation, I moved to New Haven, Connecticut, to study at Yale University, and four years later, I accepted a position as a research analyst for a social investment firm in Boston, Massachusetts. I didn't return to St. Paul until 2001, when my beloved maternal

grandfather passed away. It broke my heart. At his funeral, we displayed a painting my younger sister had created of a Hmong refugee boarding an airplane

Pakou Hang

headed towards America. Below the picture was a quote that said, "I have never left my village; now I am going to a strange country to live and die. But America will be

good for my children. They say all children can go to school there."

In the summer of 2004, I finished my first year in graduate school and traveled to Thailand to conduct research at the Wat Tham Krabok, a refugee camp that was processing Hmong people to come to the United States. The Hmong refugees at the Wat belonged to a group of 15,000 refugees who had fled the original refugee camps in 1993 after the United Nations High Commissioner for Refugees gave them an ultimatum: either resettle in the United States or go back to Laos. Many people were fearful of going to the United States yet reluctant to repatriate, especially after Mai Vue, a prominent Hmong leader, returned to Laos in May 1993 and then disappeared.

I was returning home, I thought to myself as I boarded the plane to Bangkok, Thailand. I had read stories about African Americans and Korean Americans who had traveled back to their "motherland" and found a belonging there that evaded them in the United States. Growing up, my parents had told me stories about my paternal grandfather. They had said that he was a king and I figured, if he had been a king, then I must be a princess. And I often told the rich white kids I went to school with that I was really royalty. It wasn't until I was much older that I realized my parents' limited English resulted in the wrong word choice. But the secret hope that one day I would return to our village and be welcomed like a long-lost daughter clung to my heart.

By the time I arrived in Thailand, the U.S. State Department had finished processing the bulk of the refugees and many were already preparing to leave the camp. I spent most of my time interviewing people and observing their daily activities. I also taught functional English to Hmong adults and children and visited Hmong villages in Chiang Mai and Chiang Rai, in northern Thailand. But before I left the country, I desperately wanted to visit Ban Vinai.

But returning to Ban Vinai was not as easy as I thought it would be. No one at the Wat Tham Krabok could agree on how long it would take to drive from the centrally located province, Lop

Buri where the Wat was located, to Ban Vinai situated in the northern province of Loei. Furthermore there were no major highways that led directly to the camp. I was warned that I would have to ask for directions from people on the streets. There were no major bus lines or trains that went to that area, so I would have to rent a tour guide and a van. To add complication, I did not speak Thai, which made everything seem impossible.

In his wonderful book *The Alchemist*, Paulo Coelho wrote that if a person wants something badly enough, the whole universe conspires to help her achieve her dream. And so, thanks to Si, a Hmong American from California who was working with the U.S. Embassy, we rented a van and assembled vague directions from the Hmong elders at the Wat. Three Hmong Thai women, Ma, Xas, and Bao, agreed to join us and act as interpreters. So there we were, three Hmong Americans, including my older sister who had just arrived in Thailand a day earlier, three Hmong Thai, and a Thai driver heading north to the mystical land of Ban Vinai in an old Toyota truck.

In Hmong culture, when a child enters the world, her placenta is buried underneath the place she was born, and when she dies, her spirit must go back to that place to return to the spirit world. I thought about this as we trudged up and down hills and coasted along lush green rice fields towards Loei. I kept telling my soul, remember this road, you will have to travel it again one day.

In truth, I thought the road to Ban Vinai would call to me and I would intuitively know where to turn or which path to take. But the second time we circled an intersection in Loei City, I knew we were lost. Thanks to the Hmong Thai women and some vague directions from people on street corners, we turned onto a dirt road and then to another windy road that led us past hills and flat rice fields. The terrain reminded me of the bluffs in Red Wing, Minnesota, and the fields in Iowa I had recently passed as I traveled to volunteer for a presidential campaign, before the Iowa caucuses. It wasn't long before we had to stop again to ask a couple of workers on the side of the street where the old camp with all the Hmong refugees was. One of

Ban Vinai village where Pakou Hang was born

the older Thai gentlemen, pointed at us and said, "You Hmong? You going home?" And we laughed and nodded. But I couldn't help feeling I had told him a lie. We had been driving for over 13 hours now, and if anything, the trip so far made me conscious of my yearning for the Midwest terrain. Going home? I didn't know, and that made me sad.

After an entire day driving, we finally approached the entrance to Ban Vinai. Two signs, one wooden and the other aluminum, stood at the side of the entrance, like a camp sign beckoning us in. But I didn't feel welcomed. An eerie silence permeated the air, as we drove past trees and freshly planted corn and rice seedlings. I kept waiting for the silence to be bro-

ken by the sound of trucks or children. But it remained silent, like the quiet you hear when underwater. The two signs we passed were the only indicators that this place used to be a refugee camp. Maybe there will be a plaque ahead, my sister offered. We ventured on. It was the rainy season in Thailand and the optimal time to grow vegetables. Green banana trees and green banana leaves surrounded us. Green bamboo stalks rippled down to green fields of corn and rice paddies. Green bunches of grass, some thick and bushy, others thin and sparse, lined the road. It was beautiful, but not how I had imagined Ban Vinai would look. Where were the brown grass huts and the brown trucks? Where were the people waiting to hug and welcome me home? Where were the flashes of pictures, the melody of sounds, and the array of smells locked in my spiritual and cellular memory?

We finally came upon a cement house where an old Thai man sat on the front porch. Thanks to Bao, we found out that, yes, this was Ban Vinai. No, no one lived here anymore. All the people moved away when the camp closed. There were no Hmong people here. No, he didn't know where the center of the camp was. No, none of the old houses the Hmong people lived in remained. They had all been knocked down. I did not get out of the van as Bao conversed with the old man. I could sense what he was saying, just by looking around. Ban Vinai was a ghost town. There was an

old dilapidated house where the head of the refugee camp used to live. The schoolhouse my father helped build was empty, its tin ribbed panels falling down. The old soccer field was splattered with green patches. And everything else, for miles and miles around, was just green—green trees and green corn fields. The air was muggy, even in the shade, but it smelled clean, unlike the Wat. I could not imagine 40,000 people making a life here, birthing and trying to raise families, hoping and dreaming for a better life. In this vast place, there was only silence. It was like a slate had been wiped clean and my people and I . . . forgotten.

We did not stay long at Ban Vinai. We took pictures in front of the soccer field and pictures of the famous mountain that was notorious for clandestine meetings between young lovers. But it was anticlimactic, so much less than what we had expected. In that disappointment I discovered a profound truth about who I was and what I had to let go. For me there were no jolts of deep memory. No smell or sound that I recognized. As we returned to Lop Buri, I thought to myself, in a couple of days, I will be leaving

Thailand and returning to my mom and my dad, my bed, my life in America, and that ache for home engulfed me.

There is a seduction attached to the notion of place. We imagine it as a stilled screen just waiting for us to return to reactivate it. Ban Vinai will always be the place where I was born and where my placenta is buried. But my spirit does not remain there. It is not my home. Growing up as an immigrant in the United States, Ban Vinai sustained me as all dreams do. But I discovered in returning that roots can be transplanted and still flourish. My roots are my family, my culture, and my community, and they exist in multiple dimensions, transcending several continents. I am who I am, and that is good enough. Perhaps the immigrant in me will always be searching to belong, but the Hmong in me has found her home.

Reflections on Knitting

By Nan Kari

Knit one stitch, pearl the next. It looks like this, I say, pointing to a row. Not too tight. Not too loose. Teaching these master textile artists how to knit a simple scarf is a dream, I think to myself. Of course, the Hmong women learn in a flash.

We formed a knitting circle— new knitters, old pros. It's a women's thing we say and laugh together. No translation needed here. Knit one. Pearl one. Easy enough.

How special to sit around a table in the good company of strong women knitting together. We watch each other. Eyes meet. We nod encouragement, chat in our own languages, hoping the other can catch a glimpse of the meaning we wish to communicate. Knit one. Pearl one. Scarves lengthen. Affection grows.

One evening I bring in some bawdy romance postcards—actually advertisements from an Italian restaurant where I had eaten the night before. We laugh hysterically at the slightly off-color pictures as we pass them around the circle. Now we laugh at each other's reactions. I wonder how the Hmong interpretation sounds. The rest of the hour we spend writing postcards to friends from JAS who have moved on. Imagine their surprise to find this in the mailbox, we say to each other. Kathleen will love this steamy literacy activity, I think to myself. Knit one. Pearl one.

Our friendships deepen over the months. Others join: two Mexican grandmothers, master knitters. Now we speak in three languages with lovely tones and interesting sounding words. Young daughters join. Who are we together, this eclectic group of girls and women, who have lived in such different places and know things others can only imagine?

Knit one. Pearl one. We click out a rhythm, stitching our lives together in this particular moment, in a scarf of many colors. No translation needed here.

Part Three:
TEACHING AND LEARNING

Part Three:

TEACHING AND LEARNING

"I was very skeptical of the learning culture I found at the Jane Addams School," writes Kathleen Winters, who taught French in suburban high schools for 30 years. In her essay, "The Language of Learning," she describes the journey that led her to discover the power of reciprocal teaching and learning. She transformed the professional knowledge, acquired through years of study and practice to what might be called "craft knowledge," infused with a new respect for experience, for the role of relationships in the learning process, and for the particularities of place.

To reclaim and create a democratic culture requires that we engage with one another in the exchange of ideas, knowledge, and histories. It is in these exchanges that we challenge each other to learn and develop. What does this kind of learning process have to do with democracy? Both education and democracy live in dialogue and exchange. The belief that everyone is both a teacher and a learner propels our ability to make connections with others so that together we can create a democratic environment. Our experiences and our work at JAS has helped us understand the imperative that our very freedom is bound up with our capacity to learn from others, to be open to sharing our own knowledge and experiences, and to pose new challenges that stretch and enrich us all. Learning to listen whole-heartedly is critical to building this kind of reciprocity. It requires a willingness to penetrate through early stages of incomprehension to understand the experiences as told and lived by others. It means coming to understand that specialized knowledge is valued in the life of a community, whether formally credentialed or informally acquired, as in the wisdom drawn from the values and heritage of a cultural group. In present day United States, the idea of the social construction of knowledge is in tension with our expert, status-oriented view of knowledge. We are in danger of losing our awareness that learning and also the generation of knowledge belongs to the whole people rather than to any certified, authoritative group.

Many of us—children, old-timers, college students, or new immigrants—have been schooled by systems that stifle the development of democratic habits. The place-based culture of reciprocal learning that we have sought to create at JAS serves as an underpinning for learning and relearning such habits.

Gunnar Liden, in the snapshot entitled "Elders," writes about his realization that the "real" teachers were the Hmong elders rather than Gunnar the "all-knowing"

college student. He comes to the realization that often strikes young people and college students at JAS—wisdom comes from the lived culture of a people and those who sustain it and pass it on, not simply knowledge acquired through formal education.

See Moua, too, was highly doubtful when she took on the job of coordinator of the Children's Circle at JAS. "I was programmed all my life to be organized, goal oriented, and to follow rules and procedures prescribed by others," she writes in "Children Teach Us." She tells the story of her journey of discovery to a less orderly, but far more productive way of helping children develop their own potential for leadership. The belief in everyone's capacities for public life and leadership— and a passion for developing such capacities—infused the spirit of Jane Addams's original Hull House, which JAS works to revive in our time.

See Vang's story, "The Journey," sets the stage for Terri

Wilson's account of her experiences at JAS. Eight years later, as a doctoral student at Columbia University Teachers College, Terri returned to JAS to pursue a research project. In "A Call to Vocation," she writes of what she learned at JAS about conducting research and her deepening commitment to making "research and scholarship accessible to the public . . . and directed toward public ends." She conveys a vision of scholarship tied to public purposes and conducted with public methods that are sorely needed to challenge and change our highly fragmented, privatized, hypercompetitive, efficiency-oriented society.

Nan Skelton in her essay "The Craft of Mentorship," gives us a portrayal of the reciprocal relationship aiming at development and growth that can occur in the apprenticeship/mentorship relationship. She ends with "My Eyes Big Open," a short describing the liberating impact of Phua Ly's experience at JAS.

THE LANGUAGE OF LEARNING

by Kathleen Winters

I n the beginning I was very skeptical of the learning culture I found at the Jane Addams School for Democracy because of my professional training, but in time I gained a great appreciation for it. I came to JAS having taught French for many years in a suburban high school. I wanted to gain a deeper understanding of some of the diversity issues at my school, so I signed up for a summer course at the University of Minnesota that focused on democratic education and the recent settlement of immigrants on the West Side of St. Paul. The course "lab" was JAS, where groups of Hmong and Spanish-

speaking people gathered to share culture, language, and community issues with English speakers from the neighborhood and local colleges. Much of the language learning took place through learning pairs, consisting of one English-speaking person and one non-English-speaking person. The goal for most learners was then, and still is, to practice conversation skills and develop or strengthen reading and writing skills. Little did I know then that my identity as a language

teacher—indeed, my entire perspective on teaching and learning—was about to change dramatically.

It began when I walked into a crowded room at Neighborhood House that first night and tried to figure out where I was supposed to sit. Twenty Hmong adults, mostly women, sat in small groups on children's chairs at low tables, talking animatedly and laughing as they greeted their friends. Their language, so different from my own, sounded

melodic, with held notes and tones that I knew would be difficult for me to reproduce. I found an empty chair and waited for someone to tell me what to do. I finally realized that this was not going to happen, that there would be no teacher to hand out lessons or make assignments. I could sit anywhere with anyone.

I paired up with Teng, one of the Hmong Circle participants who was preparing for the citizenship test, and helped her with some test questions: *Name the 13 original colonies. Who was Martin Luther King, Junior? Who is the governor of Minnesota? What are the three branches of government?* Along the way, I began to teach her some English. Since there were no texts, notecards, pens, and paper, I started improvising with gestures and facial expressions. At the end of the evening, I thought my communication with Teng must have been pretty ineffective. The next evening I came armed with the kinds of school supplies I use in my regular classroom. I was going to plan some *real* lessons, because surely there was a better, more efficient way to learn language than struggling in conversation. Thus, Teng and I began our journey together—she to become a naturalized citizen and I to understand language, literacy, and communication in ways I had not considered despite 30 years in the classroom. I would have much to learn.

Before coming to JAS, I had never considered what it might mean to immigrate to a high-tech, literacy-dependent society without cultural traditions of reading and writing. Many JAS participants have journeyed from East Africa, Laos, Thailand, and Latin America, where people lived in clans and close-knit villages and where the land provided their livelihood. They had little need for reading and writing. Many of the women I came to know at JAS had never even held pen or pencil. In fact, the Hmong alphabet was created only in the 1950s and the written Somali language in the 1970s. I soon discovered what it meant to come from an oral culture where everything—from complex ideas to simple directions—is communicated in verbal description and narrative, often in exquisite detail and musical intonation. As with most cultures around the world, and particularly those with oral traditions, news is passed by word of mouth through a highly effective grapevine. Short stories and folk tales served to teach lessons of values, morals, and history. JAS is rich with storytellers.

Though they support and encourage their children's education in English-speaking schools,

Teng Vang teaching Hmong language to English speakers

Kathleen Winters working with two learning partners

Hmong and East African adults have little or no confidence in their own ability to learn English. They are older adults who have lived in the United States for many years and have lived within their culture groups where they negotiate everyday life almost exclusively in their native language. They think they are too old; they're not smart enough; they don't have the time or a place to study. But little by little, seeing their own words and sentences in print and reading aloud or engaging in conversation with new and different people is a powerful experience that learning partners witness and participate in together.

In my own struggle to understand how best to teach English and citizenship to Teng, I turned to English Language Learning (ELL) and other citizenship teachers for help. After all, there seemed to be many successful adult education programs in St. Paul. I discovered, however, that most teachers had had little experience with nonliterate and preliterate language learners until recently, and many adult programs could not accept learners without some literacy experience. (Nonliterate learners have no reading or writing skills but come from a language group with a written language. Preliterate learners are those who have oral language and come from a culture in which written language does not exist or has only recently developed.)

Traditional teaching strategies for the citizenship test include using maps, time lines, word games, and matching exercises, and by categorizing information—all fairly high literacy level activities. I had to rethink how to design learning activities to accommodate preliterate learners like Teng. Through the work of national experts, such as Gail Weinstein-Shr, Elaine Aurebach, and a local teacher, Patsy Vinogradov, who have been leaders in non- and preliterate teaching and learning, I discovered a body of knowledge I could turn to and have adapted examples for the JAS setting.

One of their first and most important lessons is that engaged learning takes place in a context that has meaning. Teng and I would begin every evening with a short conversation about our families, what we did at home or at work, how we spent the weekend. We looked through photo dictionaries and Teng helped me understand what interested or frustrated her most. And so it

was that I began to discover how to identify contexts of meaning that would bring power and possibility to my partner's language learning. We used pictures from magazines and newspapers, as well as family and school photos, to support and expand our work. Over time, phrases and vocabulary from the larger cultural exchanges and political discussions became part of our learning. I didn't need to use formal language lessons after all. Just as in any well-designed lesson, our conversation included repetition, continuity, and applicability as we strengthened listening and speaking skills and began to develop reading and writing skills.

Helping Teng write and read her first sentences became a milestone for both of us. She began to initiate our conversations with her own questions. I learned about her concerns for her disabled husband and her children's progress or problems at school; she taught me about different health and healing techniques; we acted out scenarios and made our own games to help understand the citizenship questions. We worked as if in our own world. Our lives became our texts.

She and I kept a folder in which we kept summaries and examples of each evening's work. It was more a scrapbook than a text. We identified what we did in Hmong and what we did in English. It was always a good feeling to look back on what we had done and the progress we were making. Though it didn't have specific vocabulary or grammar lessons, it did capture what we were learning and how we were learning. Even though Teng might master only a few new words and phrases each time, she was building her confidence and soon began to expand her participation in cultural exchanges and to lead discussions of community issues.

A few JAS participants use the interactions with their learning partners to supplement their more formal experience in ELL classes. JAS does not compete with, nor does it intend to replace, more formal English language curricula or programs. Instead, we're building the bridge many people may need to cross before they go to a more formal educational setting.

Relationships formed at JAS can hold a significant place in people's lives; many consider JAS a gathering place for friendship as well as learning. Keeping the same learning partner from week to week not only strengthens the learning process; it also builds those relationships. Learning pairs are not always consistent from week to week, however. Although there is a core group of 25 to 30 long-term college students and AmeriCorps volunteers, people come and go as their lives dictate. Most college students stay one semester. Learners may work with two or more partners and never have enough time to build a deeper relationship or see the skill development with one partner. But many people have experienced such positive learning relationships at JAS that it is not uncommon for both English and non-English speakers to leave, only to return again after several years.

After a year of partnering with Teng, I became a literacy consultant at JAS and began to teach other English speakers, especially the college students, more strategies and tools for language learning. Drawing on my stock of language-teaching tools, I shared resources and demonstrated language-learning activities. I shared mini-lessons

they might try with the materials. I stocked the rooms with books, pictures, vocabulary flashcards, alphabet cards and games, children's books, magnetic word boards, tape recorders, and audio tapes. I tried to have interesting presentations, asked questions, and gave them time to become familiar with new language regalia. Still, I didn't feel successful.

Then one evening, I noticed Ted, a college student who had been at JAS for almost two years. During my presentations he looked bored, but there he was, working enthusiastically with his partner, using two learning activities I had showed him weeks before, mimicking the same mannerisms and comments I had used with the group. The pair was engaged in real conversation: the language concepts appeared naturally as they talked and laughed. They were creating their own lesson within a context of friendship.

Suddenly, it became clear that I had overloaded the college students with too many ideas, too many activities, too soon. The prepared lessons were more confusing than helpful because people couldn't see how to adapt the techniques to their natural

conversations, the centerpiece of paired language learning. I realized I had abandoned everything that I had learned from Teng. Meaningful context is paramount! Just as with Teng, the college students and I needed to make our own space and together create our own place within JAS. The college students didn't need to learn how to teach. It was more important for them to learn how to identify the teaching skills they already had and how they might enhance them.

The more open we became in sharing our observations and reflections, the better the college students and I were in mentoring each other; we also found we could be role models for others. I had discovered anew the power of reciprocal teaching and learning. Energized by new insights, we found an additional space at JAS for learning pairs who wanted focused help with language learning. There I ask questions, help both learning partners recognize their progress, and try to offer on-the-spot feedback and encouragement. Perhaps most important, I help them discover and uncover their own resources and creativity. Each pair takes responsibility for their own learning and chooses or creates

Kathleeen Winters (right) with Mai Yia

materials and activities that support their own work. Raising a collective awareness of the democratic learning process comes closer to the principles of JAS and we all are becoming more confident.

Learning English is a slow process and takes time, a lot of time. Because most of the participants live within their own native language cultures, they have little opportunity to practice English outside JAS. Some do practice with their children, but most have few English interactions. They may ask questions while shopping or answer a short question that doesn't require explanation, but their longest and most sustained English engagement occurs during their time at JAS.

That became clear to me when Teng and I were driving to her naturalization ceremony. Out of the blue, she quietly told me that I was the only *Mica* (American) that she ever talked to. It was a stunning and somewhat sad moment for me. I didn't want to be the only English speaker in her life. I knew the situation would change in time and it did; Teng now enthusiastically talks to everyone she knows at JAS, including people who are new to her. But her revelation made me realize just how important and life changing the learning-pair relationship can be.

In the time she and I spent together, we laughed, played games, sang, cooked, went to the library, wrote letters, read books to children, helped lead community forums, and shared family holidays. It took time and patience. But the freedom and space we had at JAS provided us our place to learn and teach together as we chose. The relationship we created in that space made it all that much more rewarding. The communication was never clearer. Trust was never more powerful.

Elders

By Gunnar Liden

Arriving at Neighborhood House that first night, I really did not know what the Jane Addams School was or who the Hmong were, nor did I have any prior English Language Learning (ELL) training.

Shortly after sitting down at a table with five Hmong women and two other college students, someone announced that we should start the "cultural exchange." The topic was the treatment of elders in society. After the facilitator announced this in English, Chong translated it into Hmong. I was amazed at the immediate commotion and conversation among the Hmong residents following the translation. The question quickly came back in English, "Why do Americans put elderly parents in nursing homes? Why would we do this if we love and respect them?" There was no room for superficial academic statements about the way things should be or how we would like to think they are. I noticed an awkward silence; none of the college students offered a straightforward answer. I was struck with a pang of guilt. While there are many reasons for the existence of nursing homes—our economic system, shrinking family size, value of individualism, time—all of these reasons sounded more like rationalizations than real answers.

The Hmong moved into the silence and then explained why respect for elders is a necessity no matter what society we belong to. I recognized the beauty of this idea. Respect for life should have no societal limitations.

I learned an important lesson that day. It happened because the space allowed for college students and the Hmong residents to talk over cultural issues in a way that valued immigrants as contributing members of our society. That evening I had not taught one thing, but I had learned something of value from those I thought I was supposed to be teaching. The idea that education can be a reciprocal activity in which everybody is a teacher and everybody is a learner intrigued me, and I sensed the potential liberation that can come from this experience.

CHILDREN TEACH US

by See Moua

"**D**on't teach the child all there is to know about life. Let the child teach you what life is all about." My good friend Kong Yang wrote this in my baby shower book more than two years ago, when I was expecting my first child. As a mother, I appreciate the wisdom of this quote more and more each day. As a professional working with children, I feel it expresses the essence of what I do, the foundation of my experiences as the coordinator of the Children's Circle at the Jane Addams School for Democracy.

I certainly didn't feel this in 2002, when I began facilitating in the Children's Circle. Unlike traditional learning environments, the Children's Circle is a loosely structured space for experimentation and ongoing creation. There are no curricula, no tests, no tidy rows of desks. Children move around freely, have a lot of say over what happens, and keep busy with many things all at once.

I was programmed all my life to be organized, goal oriented, and to follow rules and proce- dures prescribed by others. Having all these tendencies rein- forced in a state job governed by rules, I was frustrated when I began working in the seeming chaos of the Children's Circle. How could learning ever happen here when toddlers demanded my undivided attention, elemen- tary-school children tore around the room, and teens just hung out or shot hoops in the gym? How could anything productive happen when the children were randomly doing what they wanted to do?

As someone who prized order and knowing what's going to happen next, I had a hard time not wanting everything neatly arranged and planned. It was tough to let things just happen. I was used to being in charge. Over and over I tried to bring order to the chaos. Over and over, I failed. My frustration finally spilled over and I stormed into the office of codirector Nan Skelton, crying and telling her I wanted to quit. She reminded me that the Children's Circle reflected the overall philosophy of JAS—

that people of all ages learn best when they teach and learn from one another. Children and adults alike had created this space, voicing their interests and acting to make those interests a part of the circle. It was democracy at its intergenerational best.

I saw that instead of trying to fix what I thought was broken, I should pay attention to why it made me feel so uncomfortable and what I could learn from that. In time, I saw that learning was happening, even when I didn't plan it, and that learning could happen even more with the right kind of facilitation. Children could develop in remarkable ways because of the limited structure we had in place. My need to always know what was going on, to insist on order, began to subside. Before I knew it, the children were teaching me just as much as I was teaching them. I also learned that there was, in fact, a kind of structure in place though it was one that I did not immediately see. The core values of JAS provided an important framework for the work I would come to do. The lessons have been life changing.

Learning without My Rules of Order

At first, the Children's Circle wasn't much more than a handful of Hmong and Latino children coloring or playing board games with an adult or two in a small room at the Neighborhood House. About 70 children now meet each night at Humboldt High School. Although the majority are Hmong, a growing number of East African and Hispanic children participate. About 20 college students and community members work and learn with the children. Some children arrive with their parents who attend one of the adult learning circles; others come by themselves.

Based on a philosophy that recognizes that each child has unique interests, skills, and talents and that each child thinks, feels, and learns differently, the Children's Circle allows them the freedom to learn and express themselves in a variety of ways: in words spoken in the language of their choice; in recreational activities; in art, music, and dance; and in special action projects. They are encouraged to get involved through a variety of activities that they themselves help to initiate, organize, and even lead. Sports, arts and crafts, computer and board games, playwriting, choreography, and card tournaments are just a few of the relatively simple activities the children have engaged in. More involved projects have included forming an Earth Day Club, which raised funds to travel to Washington, D.C., where members met with legislators about the unfairness of the citizenship test; recording oral histories by interviewing parents and writing about their history and culture; organizing a bike marathon fundraiser to buy books for the Children's Circle; working with the Hmong Circle to pass a state resolution condemning the human-rights violations in Laos; and conducting a benefit to raise awareness about Hurricane Katrina and its aftermath and organizing drives to collect food, clothing, and money for its victims.

In contrast to conventional, overprogrammed learning environments, the Children's Circle encourages spontaneity. Our projects and activities often don't give children many guidelines for *what* to learn or *how* to learn it. At first, this style of learning confuses them. "What do you want me to do, See?" a new participant might ask me. "What would you *like* to do?" I ask in return. Most of them aren't quite sure. But after coming to the Children's Circle for a while, they quickly learn that they are capable of deciding for themselves.

Pao Fue taught me that one hot July afternoon, after he and the rest of the circle walked with me through the Humboldt High School neighborhood to photograph things we liked. When we returned to the school to develop the photos, we were exhausted from the heat. The school was not air-conditioned, and three boys fought to stand in front of the window fan to cool off. Another splashed cold water on his face at the sink in the room. I made a paper fan and began waving it in front of me. That's when I noticed Pao Fue leaving the room.

"Pao Fue, where are you going?" I called after him.

Without looking back, he shouted, "It's so hot in there, I can't stand it!"

"Pao Fue, come back—I have a fan I can share with you." There was no answer, but his footsteps stopped. I followed to see what he was doing and found him shirtless, lying on the tiled floor in the middle of the hallway and smiling.

"What are you doing down there?" I asked.

Pao Fue just grinned and said, "It's so nice and cold here."

I checked the floor for myself. Sure enough, it was.

I thought, how creative he is and how safe he feels doing something out of the ordinary like this. Would he have been as able or willing to do this in a more structured place? Or would he just have continued complaining about the heat, knowing he couldn't do much about it because of the rules he was required to follow?

Although they may not be able or willing to articulate it, children yearn to be free from other people's expectations, from simply doing what they are told, from being little adults. They yearn to be themselves and to be respected for that. Children tell me that this freedom is what makes the Children's Circle different from most other places they've been to. "You get to do whatever you want," they tell me. "You get to talk as much as you want." It's not just that they are free to act as they please; they are free to act *if*

they choose to. It's a freedom rarely found at home or at school or anywhere else in our over structured, hyperactive society.

With this freedom, they learn to take initiative, be responsible, make decisions they haven't had to make before, to question the norm, to pursue their interests, and to develop leadership and civic skills that make them proactive learners as well as productive and engaged citizens.

Learning When We Choose

When given the chance to explore a subject or activity that engages them, children not only become committed to it, they become inventive. When learning isn't forced on them, they forget to think of learning as homework or a chore, even though it might very well be both. They take risks and try new things without fear of failure. They get carried away with learning, and so do those around them.

I learned that from Chathanum, a six-year-old boy who unexpectedly joined our arts and craft group one evening. Usually, Chathanum would peek at what we were doing and then dash off, especially if the group was

made up of girls. This time, however, even though no other boys were at the art table, Chathanum stayed. Our project was to create a favorite food, vacation spot, or holiday using assorted papers, magazines, clay dough, fabrics, buttons, and sequins. He collected his materials and got down to work.

An hour later, Chathanum showed me what he had made: a three-dimensional island, complete with grass huts, palm trees, surfboards, people, even pet dogs. I asked him which island it was, thinking he'd name Hawaii, the Bahamas, or some other popular destination. "This is my favorite vacation spot!" he replied. I asked if he'd been there before. "Nope," he said.

"But if you've never been there," I asked, "how can it be your favorite spot?"

"I haven't been there, but I would like to go someday," he said. "I think I will like it a lot. There's water to play in, there's nice weather all the time, the people are kind, there's animals, and the sharks don't bite."

Wow, I thought. He knows enough about what he likes to figure out what kinds of things he would want in a favorite place. I

want to rather than because they have to?

Chanathum and others have taught me that children learn best not only when it's fun, but when someone helps them reflect on what they're learning. Critical reflection helps children make meaning of what they do and what has happened. It helps them see the bigger picture. "We like how you ask us a lot of questions," one child said to me when I asked how I could help them learn better. "It really gets us thinking."

Learning through Interaction

Interaction and play have become the heart of the Children's Circle and the reason so many participants keep coming back. Through play, children find adults and other children they want to be with. In time, children begin to trust others and develop relationships with them. Working with children means getting down to their level, being able to have fun with them, and letting them see that you are a child at heart.

I learned that lesson soon after I joined JAS. One extremely hot day, I brought the children attending our summer program to Humboldt High School's indoor

invited the other children to look at his work. "Ooh, that looks like a cool place," one said, but Chathanum cut in to say he was not quite done. He asked for more supplies to take home so he could finish the piece there.

The following night Chathanum brought his model back. His work amazed me. Waves big and small now surrounded his island, and surfers were riding them. The beach was filled with all kinds of marine life. I asked if I could show it to other people in

the room, but he said not yet. He began cutting out little white circles and placing them on the palm trees. "Are those coconuts?" I asked. "Yep," he said. "The people need food to eat." The more improvements he made to his model, the more I sat in awe of this little boy's big imagination and his devotion to his project. I thought, How often do children take projects home to finish them? How often do they remember to bring them back? How often do they do something because they

pool. Before they could get in, they had to listen to the lifeguard go over the safety rules. The building was not air-conditioned and they started to fidget in the steamy space, inching closer to the pool so that at least their feet could touch the cool water.

When the lifeguard finally allowed them to jump in, I paced along the side, counting and recounting heads, making sure I knew exactly who was where. The smell of the chlorine was getting to me, and I began to feel exhausted and sweaty. One of the girls in the pool noticed and swam over to me. "Why don't you come swim with us?" Ifrah asked. "The water is really nice."

I thought to myself, *Yes, why don't I swim? I don't have to stand here and feel miserable*. I didn't have a suit with me that afternoon, but I brought one with me the next time. More rejuvenating than keeping cool was knowing that the children loved having me in the pool with them. After we played water tag, they showed me how they could hold their breath under water and tried to beat me as we raced through the pool from one side to the other. Instead of watching them from afar, as if what they were doing was too silly for an adult to do, I was playing at their level. They began to see me as less of a teacher and more as a person they liked to be with. "Will you swim with us again next week, See?" they asked. "You've *got* to!"

The relationships children develop with each other and with adults help facilitate learning that otherwise might not happen. Children often don't want to try new things or say much to someone they don't know well or don't trust. That was the case with some older girls in the Children's Circle who wanted a space where they could talk about personal issues—dating, body image, peer pressure, getting along with their parents. When I encouraged Amanda, our new AmeriCorps member, to help them start a girls group, they didn't talk with her. At first she figured it was because she wasn't Hmong and couldn't relate well enough to them. So we invited a Hmong college student who also was new to join the group. Although I occasionally sat in on the sessions too, the girls remained quiet and the group fell apart.

The girls didn't talk much because they felt uncomfortable confiding in adults they didn't know well. We needed to spend time getting to know them first and letting them get to know us. We needed to build and earn their trust.

The same has been true in the homework group. For the first half hour, children read or do school assignments, have books read to them by college students or other adults and teens, or discuss current events or other topics in smaller groups. On a typical night, several children might shout out that they'd like help with their homework. But if I send individuals who are unfamiliar to the group, the children will tell them they're not needed. Then they'll wait up to an hour to work one-on-one with people they know.

Sometimes children ask for help even when they don't need it. Sometimes they just crave attention from caring adults they trust. This became especially clear to me one October evening when Meng won our pumpkin-carving contest. I offered him a box of prizes—small games, toys, CDs, puzzles, art supplies—saying he could pick anything as his reward for winning. After examining everything, he said, "That's it? Do you have anything else?"

A little disappointed that he was disappointed, I said, "No, Meng, I don't. Don't you like any of them?" I tried to convince him that he would be happy with the music CD *Heroes* and told him that he was my hero. He smiled, took it for a moment, then gave it back to me. I made several suggestions—candy bars, a book, a JAS t-shirt—but nothing clicked. After a long pause, Meng said, "Can we just go to Cora's again?"

Cora's is a Filipino restaurant where Meng and I once had lunch to celebrate the great job he did in helping me orient new college students to the Children's Circle. All Meng wanted as his reward for having done something well was to spend time with someone who cared about him and whom he trusted.

Learning through Families

Sometimes, when children hang out, adults at school or in the neighborhood think they are up to no good. Their parents think it's a waste of time. Hmong parents, in particular, often don't allow their children to have friends over or talk with them much on the phone. "We need space to just socialize, to be with our friends," say the teenaged Hmong boys who come to the Children's Circle at Humboldt High School. "It really helps us."

"How have you been able to convince your parents to let you come to the Children's Circle?" I asked a group of boys one night.

"We don't tell our parents that we go to Humboldt to socialize. We tell them that we go because the people there help us with our homework. We tell them we need to use the computers. We need access to the Internet to do our research papers."

"Do you tell them that we have a gym, do arts and crafts, and let you just hang out and socialize too?" I asked.

"No, because then they would-n't let us come," said one of the older boys.

Most of these things about parent-child communication in the Hmong community I have always known. Growing up in a fairly strict Hmong family, I was constantly reminded to listen to and respect my elders because they had lived longer and there-fore knew more. Often this meant I couldn't disagree with them. When I did try to express myself, they would say, "You're just a

child. You don't know anything!" Communication was not a two-way street.

It's been my experience that traditional Hmong parents typi-cally don't have conversations with their children. They don't talk about how school and life in general might be going. They are not inclined to say, "I am proud of you" or "I love you" or "You make me happy," probably because they are humble, don't want to appear boastful, and also believe that if they express such sentiments, their children may feel too self-important and possibly rebel. Talking seems to happen only when problems arise and intervention is needed.

Children working on the youth farm and market project

Sometimes, language barriers make communication more difficult. Parents don't know enough English, the language their children know best, and the children don't know enough of their native language. Sometimes, socioeconomic barriers make it hard to find time to communicate. Hmong parents often work more than one job, and their children are either in school or studying at home.

Yet Hmong parents do care about their children and think highly of them. When my colleague and I interviewed several of them through the Partners in School Change project, hoping to gauge their perceptions of their children's growth and development, Hmong parents spent hours telling us how unique and wonderful their children were. The intense concern Hmong parents feel about their children doing well in education conveys important messages for new immigrants struggling to make it in a new land. Hard work and education are seen as important in part because of the ways that such achievement can bring recognition, respect, and visibility for their families and communities, not simply to them as

individuals. Still, without everyday conversation, especially about positive things, children often don't realize the ways their parents care about them. The less time children spend with their parents, the less connected to them children feel. Many try to find caring adult relationships outside of the home, such as within the Children's Circle. That is why JAS stresses intergenerational learning and provides spaces where adults and children can work, talk, and learn together.

Learning about Leadership

Intergenerational learning not only helps bridge communication between adults and children, it also helps children develop their leadership skills—skills they usually can't learn from children who are the same age and who behave the same way. To become leaders, children need to observe role models who are older and need to become role models to those who are younger. As they interact with younger children, they learn to play nicely with them rather than look down on them. As they interact with older children and adults, they learn to respect them rather than fear or envy them.

In an intergenerational environment, children often see their parents and siblings engaged in learning. Seeing others read, for instance, encourages children to understand that reading isn't just a chore they *must* do. It's something everyone else does too, and by choice. Intergenerational learning benefits parents as well. To see their children learn makes parents feel proud. In turn, they might be inspired to focus on their own learning. In some JAS adult learning circles, children act as interpreters or tutors for their parents. Through this interaction, parents see their children more positively and value them more.

Children learn leadership skills in other ways as well, as the story of Pa illustrates. At first, this shy eight-year-old trailed behind her older sister and cousins. One day I asked Pa how she liked the Children's Circle. Like most children new to JAS, she shrugged her shoulders and said, "I don't know." I asked her what she would like to learn while she was in the group. Seeing that she was still unsure of herself, I suggested a few things—cooking, painting, playing basketball, drawing on the computer. "It's up to you," I said.

Pa's face lit up a little. "How about dancing?" she asked.

I told her we didn't have a dance group, but that we could start one if she wanted. She told me that she already knew how to dance. "That's great," I said. "Maybe you can teach me and the other children how to dance." She quickly said, "Oh no, I can't teach!" As I asked her which dances she did and how she performed them, I pointed out to her that she was teaching me. She stopped and smiled at the realization. We spent the rest of the evening talking with other children about starting a dancing group.

For the next few weeks Pa didn't come to the Children's Circle and I wondered whether she had been scared off. Just when I thought I wouldn't see her again, however, she showed up one night with a few CDs in one hand, a boombox in the other, and about five little girls behind her. "Where can we dance, See?" she asked. Pleasantly surprised to see Pa and her recruits, I arranged a space for them to dance. Checking in on them occasionally, I saw Pa dancing in slow motion at the front of the room while the others followed along. Once in a while,

she would stop the music if a girl wasn't getting it and work with her while the others continued practicing.

One night the girls told me they were ready to perform at an upcoming JAS potluck. It was inspiring to hear them explain with such confidence what they wanted to do. I asked if they would also perform at the College of St. Catherine's Asian American Festival. No, they said adamantly, they were not ready to perform for anyone other than the folks at JAS. Eventually, Pa and her growing group of peers gained enough confidence to perform for audiences outside of JAS. For some of the dances, Pa enlisted the help of her 16-year-old sister, Gao Sheng, and the mothers of the other girls to make costumes. Pa kept a log of who was in the group, how often they came, and what happened on a nightly basis when they danced.

Getting to know Pa and others like her showed me how naturally children become leaders when given the chance and the encouragement. They also need the opportunity to create leadership roles for themselves, not just to be handed roles by adults. Some children struggle with this at first,

especially those who haven't been allowed to take initiative in the past. Those children might need to have leadership roles delegated to them, usually simple ones that are easily accomplished. Then, once they build enough confidence in themselves and their abilities, the children move on to more complex roles and the natural leader in them emerges.

Learning about My Role

My role, as noted earlier, is to facilitate the Children's Circle. I thought I was going to oversee all programming and activities there, ensure that we have sufficient staff and adult participants and that these folks understand JAS philosophy and were well trained to work with children, help to promote positive youth development, and secure and distribute resources necessary for all to fully participate—all duties of typical coordinators of youth programs. But I learned that my role is so much more than that.

My role is also to build the civic life of the Children's Circle and foster an open space for creativity, organizing, discussion, reflection, and relationship building among and for people of all

See Moua and her son Joshua Xiong

children and adults to do things for themselves, to organize, and to figure out what needs to happen and how. Instead of always protecting children from making mistakes or possibly failing, I need to allow them to experiment and learn on their own. I also need to build in time for children to reflect on their learning and connect that learning to something larger. Throughout the whole process, I need to have a lot of patience and belief in the children and their potential. Being a role model and cultivating these habits in the other adults working with me, as part of the mentoring that I provide to them, make up a large part of what I do. I cannot take this role lightly, as it is crucial that more adults are on board in order to truly help children to be and to see themselves as competent, capable, and important contributors to society.

Learning about the Meaning of Our Work

Everyone does have something to contribute, no matter how old or young, educated or not educated, able to speak English or not able to say anything at all. Likewise, everyone still has something to learn. This is really what JAS is

ages, especially children. I ensure that children have ample opportunities to voice their opinions, share their skills, teach and learn from one another, organize and make a difference around issues that they care about, develop the civic skills to deliberate and work with people different from themselves, and emerge as leaders and engaged productive citizens.

This means that I have to refrain from doing what comes naturally to me, as an adult and parent. Instead of just organizing and planning everything for the children, which is quick and easy for me to do, I have to challenge

PART THREE: Teaching and Learning

all about—everyone teaching and learning from one another, in a space that is open, fluid, and flexible.

Although the work is amazing, invigorating, and a ton of fun, it is definitely hard and challenging work. What makes it so difficult is that we obviously go against the grain of current popular culture—the culture of efficiency, of doing instead of being, of programmed activities with clear outcomes but little deeper meaning, of being overscheduled, competitive, and engaged in a nonstop search for individual achievement. Today's schools function in a far different way than the Children's Circle, and convey different patterns of learning. Many Hmong parents don't support what we do since they don't see the value in open spaces for children to come learn civic skills and just be. They expect children to engage in "more productive things" like doing homework and getting good grades. Children themselves have also been taught not to question authority and to do what they've been told. They do not expect to be called upon to decide something for themselves

based on what they are feeling or interested in.

These challenges, as hard as they make my work in the Children's Circle, also motivate me to do what I do. I am not satisfied just seeing children groomed to be high achievers; I want to see them flourish in other ways. It is incredibly rewarding for me when children do blossom as a result of my pushing against the norm.

Learning about Life

Children are taking ownership of the Children's Circle and it has become their space. Children are suggesting improvements, cleaning up and taking care of our materials and supplies, teaching younger children, and helping to enforce "rules" that they created themselves. Children who were once shy are speaking up in front of large crowds and leading groups—things that they, their parents, and other adults at JAS never imagined they would do. They are actively building the circle rather than letting adults build it for them. They are shaping their learning.

The Children's Circle is truly transforming, and not just for the children. It has also transformed

me and shaped my identity as an adult, a parent, and an educator. I now see children, not in terms of what they need, but as uniquely capable beings, full of ideas, interests, and skills. I know that to help them reach their potential I must first find out who they are and where their strengths and interests lie. And I know I must allow them the freedom to do their own exploring and to express themselves in their own way.

I've learned how important play is to learning and to life and that I need to play too, especially with children. I am letting loose more, letting go of my need to think ahead all the time, and enjoying each moment as it comes. I am finding balance in how I do things as well as in how I relate to children.

I've learned that adults don't know all there is to know about life and that we often take for granted what really matters. I've learned that it is the children who help remind us what life is all about. I've learned to pull back and let them teach me a few things.

I am privileged to be their student.

A CALL TO VOCATION

by Terri S. Wilson

I remember my first year working at the Jane Addams School for Democracy as a wash of colors, languages, uncertainties, discoveries, challenges, and achievements. The challenges and achievements revolved around small things: learning to say "see you next time"; remembering a name; forgetting every other new word on the way home. Sometime that year, I volunteered to help with a project then just beginning to take shape—recording some of the stories of the community residents in the Hmong adult learning circle. I knew, by then, the outline of the story that many participants had in common: fleeing from a war, through jungles, across rivers, and to the United States. These themes had been traced across some of the *paj ntaub* (story cloth) textile work that the women had shared with me. Their stories were reflected, too, in the urgency that the women brought to their learning, in terms like *refugee, asylum,* and *camp,* which were just beginning to have meaning for me, and—most of all—in the heaviness, the weariness, and the sorrow that greeted some of my questions.

I agreed to interview See Vang, with whom I had been working for a few months. See Moua agreed to translate, and we set aside some time during our usual Wednesday night learning circle. My questions started slowly, revisiting some of the ground we had already spoken about: her children, the neighborhood, and how long she had lived in the United States. Then I asked her about her husband, how they had met, when she had gotten married. At some point while answering my questions, her gentle voice grew firmer, more insistent, and her smile faded.

She did not wait for the next question, and spoke solidly, only pausing for translation, for paragraph after paragraph.

The story spilled out in waves: fleeing with her family to Thailand; the terrible expanse of the Mekong River; the sound of gunfire; her husband's return to combat; his eventual torture and murder. It was also the story of her children: her oldest son, an adult now and still living in Thailand; her younger children from a second marriage; her reason for learning English, for leaving family behind in Thailand. What I remember most, now eight years later, was the tone of her voice: weary; full of a straight, final, flat kind of sorrow. I also remember feeling crumpled, naïve, lost. Listening to her, I had long since stopped trying to take notes. I remember just breathing, my lungs emptied, and my voice silent. I just kept nodding, over and over again, my eyes full.

From then on, my relationship with See changed. Our conversations were somehow fuller, even across our slow conversations in the broken bits of each other's language. It was easier to ask the right questions and somehow easier to really *hear* her answers. I began to get to know her sons. It became easier, and more important, to share some of my stories and photographs. Things also, indescribably, became a little lighter. As if sharing this story had made us appreciate—or even seek out—the possibility for laughter around the corner.

I did end up transcribing her story—and some of my reactions to it—for our project, but I've realized since that this project was just the beginning of a much longer and richer conversation. Since then, our paths—and our involvement in the network of learning opportunities on the West Side—have shifted, diverged, and converged again. I am now, eight years after first coming to the Jane Addams School, working on my Ph.D. at Teachers College, Columbia University. See's children are growing older, her English has improved and she is now a citizen of the United States. At the time I would never have called that long-ago conversation

This story cloth depicts stories about Hmong life in Laos.

"research" but I've realized that her story—and the many others I heard and shared while at JAS—have come to shape what I understand as research.

Two years ago, I came back to JAS for the summer, as part of a research project with parents and teachers involved in the West Side schools. One night, without a cultural exchange topic, I started to ask some of the Hmong women in our learning circle about their experiences with their children's schools. These questions, while part of my overall research project, were simple: How were they involved in the schools? Who did they usually talk to, and about what? What about these conversations worked? What was difficult? These simple questions started an animated discussion about their children's troubles in school, the difficult phone system at the local high school, and the struggles of communicating with teachers across language barriers. At some point during this discussion, See, sitting next to me, spoke about some of the problems that her son had had with truancy at the high school. Sometimes he says he is going and never shows up, she said. Sometimes he just refuses to go the school. She

paused for a minute and then said more softly, "I feel like we—the teachers and me—are trying to carry a pot full of water. We are each holding on to our side, but it is hard to walk without spilling some of the water." The conversation kept going, but the simplicity of her words,—and the eloquence of her metaphor—stayed with me. Her description of the joint task of home and school was powerful: How are we supposed to carry this child, without "spilling" him—without, in a sense, losing him—across an uneven terrain, complicated by language and difference? Through more conversations and chances to revisit this subject with See over the summer, I learned much about the hidden complexity of "parent involvement" and the sophisticated ways that parents understand their diverse roles in their child's education. My conversations with See helped to reshape the nature of the research questions I had been asking parents and teachers. Her image stayed with me through my research and writing. Sharing her image with other teachers, I was struck by its power to subtly shift their own thinking about parent involvement.

In addition to *what* I learned from See, I was deeply affected by *how* I came to learn it. Somehow, eight years later, I had circled back home—to a friendship still imbued with trust and humor, to rich conversations and discussions, to a space where my questions came alive. This circle has made me think, perhaps in new ways, about what the space of the Jane Addams School has meant to me, how it has shaped the work I do, and the person I have become.

When I remember the Jane Addams School, I mostly remember "who" it is: a community of people, linked together by a steady stream of greetings, new and accidental conversations, children ducking their heads into the room, sly jokes, and good humor. It gets harder to describe "what" it is, and easier to describe all the things it *isn't*: a building, a curriculum, a set of outcomes, a job, a role, or anything that feels anonymous. It becomes easier still to talk about "how" it happens. Here, I always remember it as a space, carefully—sometimes painstakingly—held open, full of laughter and open to ideas. This space—kept open through the efforts of many teachers, learners, colleagues and friends—was where I found my way into capacities I wasn't quite sure I had, where I tried out ideas, tested my voice, became a better listener, learned to ask questions.

I've realized that these lessons—if I can even call them that— have played a central role in shaping the work I hope to do in the world. I have come, gradually, to think of the work that I do as research. While this term never seems quite right, I have come to appreciate how what counts as research is subject to debate and discussion. With the experiences I've had as part of Jane Addams— working alongside people on problems that matter to them—I've felt more confident in taking my place in these discussions, raising objections, posing alternatives, and asking questions. Some of these questions include: How do we start with people as people, not as members of a group, sample, or category? How do we

achieve more than just "not doing harm"? What responsibilities do we have, as researchers, to confront, change, and improve the situations our research helps to

Kor Yang (left) and Terri Wilson

make clear? Who are we making these situations clear to?

To a certain extent, these questions should remain questions— a part of the hard, slow work of making our "scholarly contribu-

tions" more visible, connected, and resonant with the lives of people that we work with. In another sense, asking these questions pulls us, at least part of the way, into a response. My experiences with Jane Addams pulled me into the beginnings of my own kind of answer. I learned, above all else, that asking questions implies a commitment to respond. I've come to see that this commitment to respond can take many forms; scholars can respond to their world through thinking, writing, listening, advocating, organizing, and agitating. What these responses have in common, I think, is a commitment to make our research and scholarship public—accessible to the public, crafted with a broader public and directed towards public ends. This commitment, nurtured through my work with the Jane Addams School, has become something I can keep close to the heart of whatever work I grow into in the future.

THE CRAFT OF MENTORSHIP

by Nan Skelton

For millennia, people have been taking clay from the earth and making pots to use in their everyday lives and to adorn their dwellings.

My husband, Peter Leach, has been part of this ancient tradition. For the past 40 years, he has made thousands of functional stoneware pots that now reside in homes across the country as well as on our daily table. Peter is a 6'6" tall, lean man. His hands are twice the size of mine. When he sits at the potter's wheel, he stoops slightly, slaps a lump of clay onto the wheel, begins to gently pace the rhythm as the wheel circles, and then, with head tilted, he bends his ear toward the clay. He listens. Somewhere between his hands and his ear, the clay speaks. He discovers

what each pot will become. He is in touch with the earth and with generations of potters who have sat before similar wheels... listening.

In watching Peter, I understand the necessity of trust and relationship. Just as he trusted the clay, we at JAS trust the young people who come; and we build relationships with them in their efforts to learn, to grow, to create ideas, and to build relationships and new ways of working.

When they first come to us, many young people ask for a lesson plan, a job description, and a set of directions. They expect someone to say, "Tonight, do these three things, make these connections, build this program or project." But I hear a different question and I respond in ways they do not expect: "You will figure it out yourselves," I tell them. "You will find your own center and amazing things will happen for all of us."

It takes years to become a good potter. It took me years to learn the craft of listening, coaching, and leading.

In 1969, I had my first experience of creating and leading an organization. During the OEO (Office of Economic Opportunity) antipoverty years, I led the organizing efforts to create Oneida Community College and Helping Hand Health Center in St. Paul. I hired a staff and then set out to micromanage their creativity almost to extinction. The good news is that they figured out ways to work around me. I demanded job descriptions, work plans, time sheets, daily check-ins, weekly progress reports, and indicators of progress to meet objectives, all of my design. Why did I do it? Because someone told me that's what real managers do and I was terrified of being revealed as the fake I felt I was. I needed to be in control. I had to be the authority and my authority had to be respected. The management books I read and the people I watched reinforced this way of working. The idea that we could

be a creative group of equals learning together would take me years to grasp.

Experience taught me to recognize distinctions between management and mentorship and to embrace the latter as my preferred orientation. The young people of JAS invited me to be a guide, a companion on the journey, a source of knowledge about older (and now largely forgotten) ways of being a citizen and a public actor. It was through this shared process that I have come to understand more deeply the power and privilege of mentorship and apprenticeship.

The craft of mentorship involves a number of things. First and foremost it requires listening. Too often people listen through filters or hear what they expect to hear. As someone once said to me, "You must become your listening." Listening beyond the words has been one of the great gifts of being in relationships with people whose spoken language I do not know. As I have learned to listen with my eyes, my pulse rate, my appreciation of inflection, of the surround—sound of pain, hope, and fear—I have come to realize that if I can listen with all of me when I don't know a

person's language then I can also learn to listen in this way when I know the language. In doing so, I am a more useful and honest guide.

Second, mentoring requires opening up a space. Sometimes it is physical space and sometimes it is the psychological space that allows possibility. The promise of opportunity for creative work helps form this psychological space. Margaret Post, a doctoral student at Brandeis University and a former JAS leader, reflected on what she found helpful for her own growth:

> The critical elements for me included: a space to be creative and innovative where I could be both proactive (take initiative) and reflective about what I was doing and why I was moved to act, to exist differently in the world.

Third, it takes time, to learn *to live the questions* rather than to provide the answers. I've learned to ask questions that help people reframe issues in terms of the big picture and then invite individuals to claim their authority for addressing such issues. Young people need to know they are not detached from their histories, but part of a rich heritage of ideas and practices that have enormous

Long-time staff, college students, and others who work with immigrants at the Jane Addams School for Democracy. Front row, from left: Pakou Hang (in Wellstone t-shirt), Koshin Ahmed, Moua Xiong (squatting), Jenny Bentley, See Moua, Sara Bydzovsky, and Amanda Stoelb. Back row, from left: Derek Johnson, Mukhtar Gaaddasaar, Nan Skelton, Ted Roethke, Kari Denissen, Nan Kari, Jeff Bauer, Martha Skold, and Walter Ayala.

relevance in the twenty-first century. Because many young people experience a world that is technocratic, impersonal, and often scripted or programmed, they respond very positively to this open-ended approach.

Fourth, people live in a "place" not in a program or an organization. Therefore, it seems critical to me that our collective work is located in a real place where young people have opportunities to engage that place in visible ways. In our case it means finding place in a neighborhood where people encounter diverse languages, cultures, political worlds, and ages. Why does this matter? It is through dialogue, authentic relationships, and work in con-

95

texts like this one that we can craft a public life and reclaim our democratic roots.

Aleida Benitez, reflecting on the differences between her experience at JAS and in a previous job in Rhode Island, explained to me:

> When you are working with the community you need them to reflect back to you that you are on the right track and that the work matters. It can't just show up in reports and data sets. At JAS it was important that we web ourselves into the whole of the community rather than focus narrowly on literacy for adults.[1]

As JAS grew, we found that calling forth the creative energy and ideas from one another was an important source of power. No one individual would be the sole proprietor of the unfolding work. The creation of JAS was an ongoing lived expression of public work. At the same time it would be grounded in a dynamic conception of the person and of the individual's potential to transcend self and change the world. "The task of man, of every man . . . is to affirm . . . the world and himself and by this very means to transform both," said philosopher Martin Buber.[2]

In the mid-1980s when I was working as a public official in the Minnesota Department of Education, I was frustrated by the civil-service hiring system, which required me to create a specific employment position and then find a person to fit that position. A friend and colleague, Mike Baizerman, described an alternative system used in many European countries. They find the individual and design a position that makes the best use of the

Kari Denissen and Lia Yang

individual's skills and talents. At the time I thought, how respectful and liberating. I've never forgotten. I wanted very much for JAS to aspire to this philosophy and practice. In the main, that is how we have operated. Extraordinary people have shown up and we have created ways to support their work.

Apprenticeship of Young Leaders

We resisted even the terminology of *staff*, worrying that it placed a distance between those who were paid and those who were not, fearing this distinction would create an unwanted separation between staff members and everyone else. The typical concept of staff seemed to engender both power over others and accountability to a boss rather than accountability to the group as a whole. We wanted to create an environment where everyone could lay claim to the possibility of shared power and responsibility.

We still struggle with the language of *staff* and other labels, such as *volunteer*. Though we have not discovered an alternative language, we have found terms like *member*, *participant*, and *cocreator* helpful. Most useful is

the foundational principle that everyone has something to learn and something to teach.

During the first two years we did not have resources to hire a paid staff, which may have been a blessing in disguise. People, like D'Ann Urbaniak Lesch, See Moua, and Aleida Benitez turned up through college classes, AmeriCorps, and word of mouth. They brought energy and a kind of magic that carried a sense of the possible. We began to think of staff positions as apprenticeships in which people learned from each other and from doing. A reflective practice evolved. Regular feedback was expected and the craft of mentoring took shape as people heard their calling and met the world's invitation embodied in the immigrant children and adults.[3]

In the third year, we hired a small paid staff. We gathered around us work-study students, Page scholars, AmeriCorps members, AmeriReads students, and interns. Many came for six months and wound up staying for six years. What was it that hooked them? And more important, how was their growth fostered? In part, it was the weekly meeting in which they were

called upon to contribute; it was the relationships they formed with the families and with other young people; it was the mentoring and coaching they received on a regular basis; it was the value others placed on their contribution and participation. And it was the daily opportunity to create a public space, rare in their experiences elsewhere.

Structures for Mentoring

I established a practice of coaching and reflection with the core JAS leaders. This proved an important part of our collective growth and practice. We structured the conversation in ways that helped people prepare for the next week's work. For example, in weekly visits, D'Ann Urbaniak Lesch would tell me the things she felt good about, a current problem she was struggling with, and a problem she anticipated. We would then, together, reflect, come up with ideas, and work at finding alternate solutions. In the course of the dialogue a lot of movement occurred. I wasn't telling her what to do. We figured it out together. I found that it was important for both of us to have a space where we could bring out worries and anxieties and celebrate little achievements. The mentoring was not one-way. It became a two-way commitment, attended to and prepared for by each of us. Each time we came together, I learned from her the meaning of my work. Our weekly meetings served this purpose for me. In time, she recognized that this process aided her own learning and growth. Now she guides those she works with in similar ways.

Because D'Ann has been with JAS since 1998, I have been privileged to witness her growth and development over a long period of time. She has become tenacious in her attentiveness and appreciation of the wholeness of people, helping others to grow out of their one-dimensional views. She has learned the political landscape through the eyes of new immigrants; she has learned the limitations of the social-service mentality in the JAS context, but won't abandon people when she sees how many needs they have. She sees challenges and has many concerns but always derives energy from being with people. She has learned to deal in a gentle way with the homely but complex task of getting a group of people

to clarify their purpose, lay plans, return with progress updates and lay out the preparations for the follow-up stages, and she has struggled successfully with how to do this without taking control away from the group.

Over time, D'Ann responded to what JAS called her to be and in answering this call, she became a chief architect of the school, always including more and more people in the ownership circle.

Mentoring as Democratic Practice

It takes time to move from the *concept* of democratic practice to actual engagement in these practices. Moreover, in our society, infused as it is with the language of highly professionalized "helping" that can undermine people's capacities for self-initiated action, it takes sustained effort to realize the organizing adage: never do things for people that they can do for themselves. Mentoring staff members in ways that free them from following a playbook of techniques rather than finding and unleashing their own and others' creative power, allows us all to deepen our democratic practices. Over the last several years, I have observed the chil-

dren of JAS work on issues, learn how to take action, and develop the confidence and skills to do so.

See Moua spent two years reflecting on her efforts to engage the children in democratic practices. She wanted them to experience making decisions, sharing ideas, negotiating turns, and respecting the different choices their peers made. Often she came away feeling frustrated. But over time, the children began to realize that they could work on things that mattered to them. One day a group of eight-year-old girls asked See, "If we have a good idea, can we make it happen?" The answer? "Of course!" And a dance troupe was born! The mentoring See experienced was now taking root in the children.

As we invite each other to discover our own capacities for action—to bring forth the ideas, the content of our activities, the problems needing attention and shape, the decisions of the day— people gradually begin to step up to the work of creating a democratic system and the realization of their own agency. It is hard work because it doesn't come naturally. The default is to fall back into old top-down habits, which are often more comfortable.

Aleida Benitez with children

One result that characterizes the difference between a traditional bureaucratic organization and this kind of mentorship is the liberation of creativity. In the early days, it seemed natural for Aleida Benitez to ask what she should do and wait for an assignment. The expectation, sometimes held by both of us, was that I should have a plan, and if she followed it, good things would happen. When I asked instead what *she* thought we could do, remarkable things resulted. In time she stopped asking me and instead told me with great enthusiasm the new adventure she was going to try with the children. Her enthusiasm alone often made the ideas work. Once the freedom to create took hold the ideas tumbled forth. Eventually there were so many things going on we had to find more and more people to join the parade. Aleida recalls:

> The JAS environment was authentic. As students we were asked to participate in this space by creating it together. . . . "We want you to be real, we want you to be present. There is no recipe to do this, yet." It wasn't just throwing people out there. . . sink or swim. . . . Hands supported me not in the actual nitty gritty; there wasn't someone there to help me get the paint, but there was always someone there to help me see the bigger picture, to reflect, to give encouragement. This gave me the confidence to try new things.[4]

When Aleida began asking the children to make decisions and plan what and how they wanted to learn, teach, and create, they started to see JAS as theirs, too. In the words of Myles Horton, the founder of the Highlander Folk school in New Market, Tennessee, we "*make the road by walking*." The JAS children learned the traditions and practices on which they were building. What I learned from Aleida, the children, and so many others was the extraordinary possibility within each person.

Individuals have the capacity to make sense out of the world, to craft a public life, to live on the basis of meaning, not just of needs, and to see themselves as part of a living democratic culture and heritage. People who are attentive to the world can see the world, appreciate differences, and commit themselves to making things different through personal choice and group action.

The mentoring relationship can be helpful to people as they explore their unique talents and find their vocations. When Aleida reflected with me about her experience, she explained that this mentoring relationship was not one-dimensional. She recognized that I saw her as more than just the student or the employee: I recognized and honored her multiple roles and talents.

> The relationship was not about a job, but about common work. . . working together for a greater good. It has not been limiting. It is constantly about growth and learning. It is not demanded that these things get done, but encouraging growth as a person and as a leader. Being asked to see myself as a leader. You validated me; you told me I could be a great leader in the community. I kind of went along with it but I didn't believe it until much later. You saw in me what I couldn't see in myself . . . for another five or six years.[5]

Conclusion

The potter listens to the clay on the wheel. The pot is already there in the clay. . . . It only needs to be drawn forth. It is an ancient craft. As I sit around a wheel-shaped table in my office, reflecting on the craft of mentoring, I know I have responded to a call.

Several principles capture some of what I have learned in this work, about the development and mentoring of young public leaders:

- Hold true to the practice that you and everyone else are both teachers and learners.

- Understand that being in relationship is the heart of the process.

- Create multiple spaces for people to be creative and self-directed; challenge people to be proactive.

- Develop the art and practice of reflection.

- Live values not standards. Rarely think in terms of mistakes. This is *really* important . . . and *really* hard. At the same time, it is important to be able to reflect honestly on what went wrong and how things can be improved.

- Establish a culture of mutual accountability.

- Offer multiple opportunities for people to be challenged by groups and experiences outside their own worlds.

Of particular importance is to infuse this work of mentoring young public leaders with a strong and active sense that people's efforts *matter* in their immediate circles and to the larger world. It is all too easy, in a world full of destructive trends and overwhelming problems, to imagine that we can create a safe enclave apart from the world.

JAS presents an alternative culture, one full of resources and possibilities for engaging and transforming the larger society. Through the craft of mentorship, we discover not only individual potential but also what our democratic society can become. The young people whom I have seen grow and develop here give me hope, because they have the potential to be architects of broad, important changes in the work of democracy.

[1] Aleida Benitez, interview, March 2005.

[2] Martin Buber, *The Way of Man* (Secaucus, NJ: Carol Publishing Group, 1998), 6.

[3] Michael Baizerman, "The Call to Responsible Selfhood: The Vocational in the Lives of Youth" (unpublished).

[4] Aleida Benitez, interview, March 2005.

[5] Ibid.

My Eyes Big Open

By Nan Skelton

In 1997, Plua Ly begins her connection with the Jane Addams School for Democracy. Her first night she sits at a table with ten other Hmong adults. She is given a pencil and for the first time in her life attempts to print her name. The pencil breaks, announcing her fears, embarrassment, and certainty that she will never be part of this strange land.

She left her village in Laos with her family in 1976. She walked through the jungle, swam the Mekong, gave birth to a third child, arrived in the refugee camp, lost a child, birthed another, flew to the United States, and encountered a fast forward to a new century. Grief, loneliness, and depression tried to break her spirit.

I met her soon after she came to Jane Addams School. Our friendship grew as I helped her understand the U.S. political landscape and learn the intricacies of the U.S. citizenship test, and she showed me how to communicate and grow a friendship when you don't share a language or culture. As time went on, she took on leadership roles, served on the Humboldt School Site Council, taught Community Education classes, worked for political candidates, and voted.

One night driving home in the dark from Jane Addams School, Plua filled the silence with her reminiscences of the years she stayed home crying, afraid to leave her house, a prisoner in another time and space. And then, from her rider's seat a few inches from me, she blurted out, "I am so happy!" Startled, I said, "I'm glad. . . . But why?" Her answer: "My eyes big open, now!"

Part Four:
EXERCISING DEMOCRACY

Part Four:

EXERCISING DEMOCRACY

Jane Addams' visit in 1888 to the first settlement located in the East London neighborhood, was a revelation for her. Toynbee Hall, then four years old, presented an alternative to the religion-based charity approach to relieving poverty that Addams and her peers had begun to question. At Toynbee Hall, university men worked with the poor; in exchange they gained a sense of usefulness and an understanding of how social classes mixed in society, while avoiding the professional "do good" attitudes of organized charity work, typical of their time.

Gertrude Himmelfarb, an American historian known for her studies of the intellectual history of the Victorian era, writes of this radical model:

> *It was meant rather to be a civic community, based upon a common denominator of citizenship in the largest sense of that word, a citizenship that made tolerable all those other social distinctions which were natural and inevitable, but which should not be exacerbated and should not be permitted to obscure the common humanity of individuals. The settlement house was not an experiment in socialism; it was an experiment in democracy—which was no mean feat at that time and place.[1]*

To understand the values of democracy and to put them into practice requires diverse public settings—in Himmelfarb's term, a civic community. This nine-

---

[1]Quotation cited in G. Dilberto, *A Useful Woman: The Early Life of Jane Addams* (New York: Lisa Drew Book/Scribner, 1999), 130-131.

teenth-century ideal, although originating at a very different time in history, continues to inspire. To learn civics through an academic curriculum or in preparation for the citizenship test is not enough. People learn about democracy by practicing it. Change occurs when people work together—making connections, building networks, doing politics.

The final essays in this collection examine some of these ideas and practices carried out at the Jane Addams School. Pakou Hang tells the story of JAS participants who launched a campaign to raise the visibility of the human-rights abuses of Hmong people in Laotian jungles. What began as a plea from one participant in the Hmong Circle grew into an initiative that influenced the thinking of state and national leaders. If the campaign was ultimately unsuccessful in changing the wording of a particular congressional bill that was its target,

the rewards were nevertheless manifest to those who participated in the effort. "We are agents of change," said one woman. "My world is growing," concluded another.

A giant figure in that world was Minnesota senator Paul Wellstone. The poignant "snapshot" produced by Nan Skelton portrays the grief we felt over his death in 2003. Senator Wellstone and the immigrant families at JAS held each other in high mutual regard. The senator's core message that "politics is for the improvement of people's lives" resonated with all of us and continues to energize us to think about our collective agency.

It is through action that people come to appreciate the notion that citizenship means more than legal status. They participate in public life in multiple ways, and, in so doing, develop civic identities. In the conversation entitled "A Civic Community," Koshin

Ahmed, a recent Somali immigrant reflects on his perceptions of the Jane Addams School as a community where East Africans experiment with the ideas of democracy. Eduardo Jurado writes about his encounter with democratic values as a South American in "Bridging the Americas." One of the gifts of the Jane Addams School experiment has been the ongoing discussions about democracy from very different points of view.

In the final essay, Nan Kari examines the nature and value of campus-community relationships. Although the partners that support the JAS work have struggled to learn how to cross the neighborhood-academic cultural borders, there are important resources for both higher education and the neighborhood when people work on issues of public concern. In the process, civic cultures in the academy and the community are strengthened.

BUILDING A POLITICAL CONSCIOUSNESS

by Pakou Hang

Mai Yia heard about the public meeting at Central High School from her husband, who had heard about it from his cousin. Nan read about it in an e-mail sent by a former graduate student. And Moua heard about it from his friends in the Hmong Student Association at the University of Minnesota. A self-appointed fact-finding commission invited community members to Central High School, where a video about the plight of Hmong families trapped in the jungles of Laos would be shown.

Mai Yia, Nan, and Moua did not see each other when they arrived at the high school. The 2,000-seat auditorium was filled to capacity, mostly with older Hmong men in camouflage army uniforms. Throughout the presentation, people listened intently as commission members spoke about the atrocities they had witnessed in the jungles of Laos. They showed video clips of starving Hmong children with bloated bellies, armless Hmong men mutilated by hidden land mines, and emaciated Hmong women nursing babies who looked like tiny skeletons.

Three days later in the Hmong Circle at the Jane Addams School for Democracy, Mai Yia told the story of the commission's findings and urged her peers to do something about the unimaginable situation. "If the pictures do not bring tears to your eyes," she said, clutching a Kleenex tissue, "then you are not a human being." This compelling story, it turned out, touched the lives of many JAS participants. It inspired a remarkable project ultimately

involving the whole of JAS and culminated in the passage of a resolution signed by the Minnesota state legislature. The public work required to accomplish that task provides an interesting account of the power people can generate as they develop a political consciousness.

I came to JAS in the summer of 2003, passionate about questions related to how people who do not see themselves as powerful, develop political consciousness. My belief that immigrant groups can build a collective sense of political power was fueled in part by the successful election of Mee Moua, the first Hmong state senator in the United States. I managed her campaign in 2001. Though we felt we were novices in the sophisticated high-tech world of electoral organizing, we had a sense that our work was real and that it mattered. "This is history in the making," we frequently told each other. I saw how including disenfranchised communities in a campaign plan—clarifying basic logistics about voting and providing interpreters at polling sites—could turn out a record number of new voters and ignite a fire in an immigrant community.

In the end, we concluded that the successful campaign rested on a few principles very much congruent with Hmong community values: Treat elders with respect; use social networks; rely on the community to give direction. We found that we could apply these values in new settings and that they are in fact at the core of successful grassroots organizing. For me, the campaign experience generated a sense of hope and new questions about how new Americans come to see themselves as effective public people.

When Mai Yia posed the prob-

State senator Mee Moua, center right, presents flowers to new citizens.

lem described by the photojournalists to members of the Hmong Circle, I wondered if we could generate a sense of urgency and possibility similar to that which prompted hundreds of people to vote for Mee Moua, but to do so in a context other than a political campaign. Specifically, I wondered if the Laos campaign could

become a medium for people to develop a sense of agency.

The human-rights abuses in Laos and the continuing struggle of the Hmong revealed an issue of injustice that many people cared about, and it provided a context in which to raise political awareness among participants at JAS. To understand the complex issue, people needed to know a little about the history of the Hmong alliance with the United States during the Vietnam War and the political drama that had taken place at the state level, as well as those unfolding in Congress. Success for our project required understanding the political landscape—past and present.

The Hmong Role in the Vietnam War

Hmong people are an ethnic minority group originating in China hundreds of years ago. Prior to the Vietnam War, the Hmong lived in Southeast Asia in Thailand, Laos, Cambodia, and Vietnam. For the Hmong in Laos, life was harsh. Forced to walk on their knees when passing Laotian lowland villages and barred from schools and positions of power, the Hmong mostly kept to themselves, working the land as subsistence farmers and growing opium for the illicit heroin trade. In the 1950s, scrimmages between the neutralist Royal Lao Army and the pro-Communist *Pathet Lao* spilled into the Laotian mountains where the Hmong people lived. In 1960, U.S. president

Dwight Eisenhower approved a CIA proposal to secretly train and arm Hmong soldiers to fight Communist insurgents in Laos. These actions were hidden from the American public. Under the military leadership of General Vang Pao, Hmong soldiers were ordered to disrupt activities along the Ho Chi Minh Trail and to search for, and rescue, fallen American pilots in the Laotian Plain of Jars.* Known as the Secret War, the alliance between the CIA and the Hmong lasted from 1960 to 1975, prior to and during the Vietnam War.

On January 27, 1973, officials from the United States and Vietnam signed the Paris Agreement to end the Vietnam War. One month later, representatives from the former neutralists and Communist factions also signed a cease-fire in Laos, which ushered in a new coalition government. The coalition government remained intact until 1975 when the Communist faction, the Pathet Lao, orchestrated a coup, seized power, and declared Laos a Communist state. At the same time, the Pathet Lao began rounding up former Hmong sol-

diers and Hmong families, detaining them in "reeducation camps." Survivors tell horrendous stories of human abuse: starvation, rape, torture, and impalement.

Early in 1975, Hmong villagers secretly began to flee Laos to seek asylum in refugee camps in Thailand. Between 1976 and 1996, over 150,000 Hmong from the Thai refugee camps resettled in the United States. While many Hmong emigrated, a small number fled into the jungles of Laos and have remained. Their dire straits surfaced in a dramatic public way in 2004, through revealing photographs and firsthand accounts.

Normalizing Trade with Laos

According to the 2000 U.S. census, Minneapolis and St. Paul have the largest concentration of Hmong residents of any metropolitan area. The economic boom of the mid-1990s accounted for record numbers of Hmong buying homes and starting new businesses. With the election of Mee Moua in 2001, the Hmong community felt they had a stronger voice in policymaking.

---

*The Plain of Jars, situated in a remote area of Northeast Laos, is one of the most important ancient sites in Southeast Asia. Scattered over an area of several square miles are hundreds of large urns made of stone. Little is known about why they are there or who created them.

Several months later in 2002, the Hmong community was again pivotal in a highly contested Minnesota race that could determine control of the U.S. Senate. St. Paul mayor, Republican Norm Coleman, had challenged Democratic incumbent Senator Paul Wellstone. Wellstone had been the senate sponsor of the Hmong Veterans Naturalization Act that passed in 2000, which allowed elderly Hmong veterans and their wives to take the U.S. citizenship test in Hmong. As a result, more than 4,000 Hmong people nationwide became citizens. Consequently the Hmong community felt great affection for Paul Wellstone. His unexpected death on October 25, 2003, devastated the Hmong community and culminated in an even greater turnout on election day. According to the Minnesota secretary of state's records, the number of Hmong voters grew from a previous 2,000 to more than 11,000. Voter turnout in some Hmong precincts had increased by more than 80 percent. The Hmong community emerged as a serious political voting block— a force to be reckoned with for St. Paul elected officials.

In the fall of 2003, U.S. congresswoman Betty McCollum of the Fourth Congressional District, which includes St. Paul, Minnesota, introduced a bill to normalize trade relations with Laos. Acknowledging gross human-rights violations in Laos, she concluded that the best way to change Laos was through active trade engagement. Angering many of her Hmong constituents, however, she refused to include a human-rights stipulation in her bill, arguing that such a stipulation would kill the bill before it could get off the House floor. Opponents of the bill, including many former Hmong military leaders, claimed that any engagement with Communist Laos would only fill the coffers of the corrupt government and increase the resources used to persecute Hmong people.

About the time Congresswoman McCollum introduced the bill, commonly referred to as NTR, a Hmong minister, the Reverend Karl Moua, went to visit his relatives in Laos. There he was arrested and imprisoned on allegations of trespassing. Moua claimed that he was acting as an interpreter for two European photojournalists who were

A discussion with U.S. senator Paul Wellstone

investigating the rumors of Hmong people living in the jungles. Reverend Moua's incarceration and subsequent release after intense media scrutiny and intervention from the U.S. State Department fueled even more opposition to normalizing trade with Laos. Despite the escalating economic debate, little effort was made to assess the welfare of the people in question or to inquire about their interests.

JAS Steps In

When Mai Yia made her presentation to the JAS Hmong Circle, people were both moved by the deplorable situation in Laos and apprehensive about getting involved. We knew that the problem was complicated by multilayered politics involving U.S. and Laotian relations, Hmong military leaders in the U.S., and Hmong factions in Laos. With all the political camps, it was hard to read the situation. We were acutely aware that, in the past, supporters had tried to help the Hmong in Laos but were later criticized for raising hopes without accomplishing any real

Three hundred people showed up to talk with their legislators and other leaders about the need for a bill that would allow the Hmong to take the citizenship test in their own language. From left to right, behind the table, are the late Senator Paul Wellstone, Neal Thou, a St. Paul school board member who acted as an interpreter, and U.S. congressman Bruce Vento.

change. We did not want to raise false hopes, but a deep sense of urgency permeated our discussions. According to the photojournalists' presentation, people were on the brink of starvation; waiting even a few months could mean life or death. The sense of urgency fueled new energy. Thus began a process involving several phases from which we learned what a small group of people could accomplish.

Fact Finding. Mapping the politics was the first step. As

with most political change efforts, larger events dramatically shape work at the local level. In this instance unfortunately, Congresswoman McCollum's NTR bill exacerbated a polarized situation within the Hmong community divided by those who saw the bill as a door into the growing Laotian market and those who were strongly opposed to the Communist Laotian government and used the rhetoric of human rights to attack it. JAS participants had to be careful in framing their position in order to avoid being pulled into either political camp. Part of the learning involved navigating the ideological enclaves.

A working group formed to research the issue, determine strategies, and identify key stakeholders. Some people investigated the application of international and human-rights laws and found out which protocols Laos had signed. Others reviewed past U.S. trade agreements with other developing countries to see how allegations of human-rights violations were handled. We interviewed community stakeholders to determine their views about the issue and their thoughts about resolving it. We collected and transcribed stories from JAS participants who had relatives currently living in Laos.

Within two months, members of the working committee had compiled a fact book that outlined various perspectives on the issue and included articles from local, national, and international media regarding the human-rights abuse. Mee Chang, a student at the College of St. Catherine, helped organize a letter-writing campaign among Hmong participants. Erik Skold organized teenaged Hmong boys to interview their parents and relatives about

life in Laos. Chy Ly, a university graduate student, interviewed Hmong adults and translated their personal testimonies to include in the fact book. Joel Ulrich, another graduate student, found out that Amnesty International and other international nongovernmental organizations were equally concerned about the situation. Ted Roethke, a Macalester College student, discovered that in a previous economic trade bill with Vietnam, the United States had included a human-rights stipulation to protect the Montagnard people in Vietnam. As the working group discussed and weighed this information with circle participants, a preliminary JAS goal emerged: to persuade Congress to include a stipulation in the NTR bill that would link trade with improved human rights in Laos.

Strategizing. It seemed like a straightforward idea—link economic trade with human rights. The State Department had long known of Laos's deplorable record and the goal of engagement was to entice Laos to change its ways. But tying human rights to an economic trade bill proved far more complicated than anticipated.

After the working group put

together the fact book, we invited Reverend Karl Moua and Congresswoman Betty McCollum to talk with JAS participants about their positions on the Hmong people in exile. Reverend Moua spoke to a roomful of over 150 people, recounting his ordeal in Laos and telling the audience of other Hmong prisoners he had met while in jail. He spoke about the inhumane prison conditions and the many false allegations commonly made against Hmong men in Laos. Reverend Moua also asked JAS participants to sign a petition to get a hearing with the United Nations' Anti-Discrimination Committee. He encouraged the working group to connect with other international organizations that were also concerned about the Hmong in the jungle.

Representative McCollum did not come but sent her Hmong legislative assistant, Chao Lee. Mr. Lee spoke about the need to engage Laos in economic development and trade and said that a sizable, albeit quiet, segment of the Hmong community wanted to open up trade relations with Laos. In a roomful of mostly Hmong elders, Mr. Lee explained that the allegations of human-rights abuse in Laos were grossly exaggerated and that the Hmong people could leave the jungle to join mainstream Laotian society if they chose. His position and his unwillingness to hear other perspectives fueled some animosity between JAS participants and Representative McCollum's office.

In the debriefing session that followed, many elders expressed frustration that Representative McCollum's office clearly did not welcome other perspectives. If she wouldn't listen, who would? Seeking a larger and more diverse base of support, the working group decided to engage members of other JAS learning circles, anticipating that people from other countries may have had similar firsthand experiences with U.S. involvement in wars in their regions. Indeed, Latinos from Central and South America readily understood the situation. Members of the East African Circle, many of whom were also political refugees, expressed solidarity. They too had fled their war-torn countries and had family members who were now targets of reprisal by nondemocratic regimes. Having discovered a common theme among many JAS participants, the question now became how to organize an action.

Taking Action. Mee Chang organized a letter-writing campaign among Hmong participants to local newspapers and ethnic presses. Another JAS organizer arranged for a meeting with three Hmong women and their state representative, John Lesch, who represented the area of St. Paul with the largest Hmong neighborhoods. At the meeting, the women told him about their families in Laos and the sporadic news they received about police brutality. They showed him the fact book created at JAS and discussed their concerns. "We are agents of change," concluded one of the women after the meeting. Representative Lesch's affirmation reinforced the sense that "my world is growing," as Chao Moua said. Indeed, developing a public and political identity involves seeing new, larger connections and possibilities. It means learning to engage in situations of political ambiguity, where allies and opponents shift constantly. Ideological categories are not sufficient. Lesch encouraged JAS participants in their efforts to increase public awareness by organizing an event at the state capitol and offered his assistance.

The committee decided to submit a resolution to the Minnesota legislature. Working with the University of Minnesota Human Rights Center and state representatives John Lesch, Cy Thao, and state senator Mee Moua, we crafted a resolution that condemned human-rights violations in Laos and urged the Laotian government to allow nongovernmental organizations into the jungles to assess the situation as neutral observers and give medical treatment to those in need. We also prepared a briefing memo outlining key findings and recommendations, which we distributed to all the state legislators and faxed to local mainstream and ethnic media outlets. We invited all JAS participants, past and present, from every language circle, citizens and noncitizens, as well as allies, such as Progressive Minnesota, the Immigrant Workers Freedom Ride, representatives from the Asian-American Council, and staff from the offices of U.S. senators Mark Dayton and Norm Coleman, to a press conference where we unveiled the resolution.

We held the press conference at the state capitol and conducted it in Hmong and English. In front of a standing-room-only crowd, Mai Yia presented her testimony in Hmong (followed by an

Minnesota state representative John Lesch (first from left, back row), St. Paul mayor Chris Coleman (second from left, back row), and state senator Mee Moua (at far right, back row) pose with JAS students and friends.

English translation), and Chao Moua made a statement on behalf of the youth political group. After other elected officials spoke, the floor was opened to comments from the audience. JAS participants and others shared personal accounts of family members unable to escape from their jungle existence. It was a powerful public experience. Major newspapers and radio stations in the Twin Cities and three major ethnic presses covered the event. Later that day, the resolution unanimously passed in the state legislature.

Conclusion

Shortly thereafter, Mai Yia was asked to appear on a college radio show because of her eloquence in addressing the cause. She was apprehensive at first and asked why she had been chosen from among all the other Hmong participants in the circle. Her learning partner, Ted Roethke, told her: "We didn't select you, you chose yourself. You stood up when others didn't."

In this story, many people—citizens and noncitizens alike—played active roles. Some who were nonnative English speakers felt passionate enough to transcend their fear of not speaking fluent English or not being legal citizens in order to act in public

A CIVIC COMMUNITY:

An Interview with Koshin Ahmed*

VOICES OF HOPE: The Story of the Jane Addams School for Democracy

The following interview with Koshin Ahmed, a Somali immigrant who is a facilitator and interpreter for the East African Circle at JAS, was conducted and edited by JAS codirector Nan Kari.

Kari: *What impact does participation at JAS have for Somali people who are part of the East African Circle?*

Ahmed: I come from a country where the concepts of democracy, citizenship, and community and their values are not practiced. Somalia is one of those rare nations with very few or no differences in terms of culture, religion, language, and ethnicity. There is little or no room for individual thought or self-reflection. This leads the majority of people who grow up there to think we have no differences; therefore, our individual and social interactions are based on that perception. Native Somalis are not aware of individual and collective rights and freedoms, because no Somali government has ever truly promoted a constitutionally based democracy, where free association is encouraged. Consequently, democracy and citizenship have always been abstract concepts in Somali culture.

Even the idea of community is new to many Somalis who now live in the United States because of our homogeneous political and historical backgrounds. What is missing in Somali culture is the heterogeneity I see here in America—not racial heterogeneity per se, but the different ways in which people think and express themselves.

When Somalis come to JAS to participate in the circle, they have a chance to voice their political, social, and religious viewpoints. I encourage them to speak their minds. This is especially important for the women. I see them struggle to voice their opinions. They want to say something, and it is hard for them to say it constructively because they are not familiar with community-based discussions. There were no community organizations like JAS in Somalia. Women have also been underrepresented in many public activities in Somalia. In addition, most of them did not go to school, so they have not participated in formal or academic discussions.

Certain ideologies have existed for centuries in our society that favor male dominance. Women have stayed home to be in charge of the house and children. They

---

*The interview took place at the University of Minnesota on December 22, 2004, and January 11, 2005.

might not go to school or pursue careers because it is assumed they will marry and become mothers, which ultimately leads them to continue house chores. There is a saying in Somalia that goes, "A woman is a woman," which literally means that whatever career a woman might pursue won't last long. (I'm not discontented with my culture. I'm simply sharing some of the obstacles Somali women face on a daily basis.) Here in the United States, Somali women have more options and flexibilities for learning comparative roles that are useful, both for them and the community at large.

Kari: What approaches, have you found, facilitate these community-based discussions?

Ahmed: The JAS setting gives every one of us Somalis and natives* a chance to teach others about ourselves and to learn from everyone else in the group. The setting provides a hospitable space for our learning circles. The questions and the topics we discuss allow us to share how we see ourselves and our cultures. When the group engages in dialogues about culture, we learn by talking

Koshin Ahmed

with each other, not at each other.

One night during our cultural exchange, the East African Circle included Somali women, with some dressed in traditional religious clothing, and students from the College of St. Catherine, some dressed casually in jeans and shirts with their hair uncovered. At the end of the discussion, the students said to me they would like to ask why some Somali women cover their faces almost entirely and others only cover

---

*Ahmed uses the term *natives* to refer to U.S.-born citizens.

their hair and wear Western clothes. The next time we met, everybody talked about clothing. Somali women asked many questions about why American women do not cover their hair. In earlier days, they said, American women used to cover their hair and most of their body. Why had things changed?

This curiosity and freedom to ask and answer questions helps us get to know and understand each other better. Inquiring about the *hijab* (scarf) is just the opening to deeper conversations. When American students inquire about the Somali traditional clothing and related cultural things, for example, the answers almost always have to do with religion. In the East African Circle, most of the participants are Muslims or Christians. In Somalia, religion and state are almost a single institution; in the United States, they are separate institutions. Natives have their own way of expressing their opinions without referring to a religion, whereas Somali participants have difficulty expressing themselves apart from their religion. Each one of us implicitly realizes our differences in religion and lifestyle and worldviews, but those differences become more visible when you are part of a heterogeneous group.

This is the thing I like about America. You can always be kept in check by encountering people who are different. Seeing those differences creates the opportunity to see what we are not, but in a positive way. When you learn who you are not, you realize who you are. I never thought this way when I was living in Somalia, because it is such a homogeneous society.

Kari: Have you found ways that help diverse people to know each other as individuals?

Ahmed: When people come into the circle, the first thing we do is introduce ourselves, despite the fact that most of us already know each other's names. Second, we inquire of each other what we have done in the last week. With this introduction, we create an immediate shared reality—we connect to one another by sharing the basic things we do

every day. I have seen native students sometimes feel stressed when they are asked to partner with someone like the elderly immigrants who don't speak English. They don't know how to approach them. Sitting close together, facing each other, creates a kind of communication that goes beyond words. After a while, they become enmeshed with their learning partners and develop their own way of communicating with them. They learn together and teach each other's cultures, languages, and traditions, despite the language barrier.

When we can hear the tone of our voices and sense the emotions in our stories, we give each other some idea of who we are. It is hard to understand a story deeply if you haven't experienced it. It is hard to walk in someone else's shoes. One time in our group, I shared a story about living in a refugee camp, where many of us became desperate about the situation. We would wake up in the morning and have nothing to do: no school, no job. Everything that sustains life was either scarce or could not be found. However, every morning I woke up believing one day I would go some place where I could go to school

and live a better life. I never lost hope. The native students in the group witnessed my story in a different way, but as they heard my voice and saw my face, they felt some of what I had felt.

Another night in the East African Circle we asked people to tell a meaningful story about their lives and families. Raymond, who is from Liberia, shared his story about the war in his country and how he survived, even though many of his relatives did not. He told us he witnessed his father killed with a machete by the rebels. The expression of grief on his face was so great that we could not help but imagine what he was feeling. There was no way we could experience what he saw with his own eyes, but we had the ability to be with him in his remembering.

New students from the College of St. Catherine were in the group that night. Kate, a professor who came with them, shared a story that was similarly profound and touching. Her story was about the time when her mother was dying. Kate said that it was important that she and her daughter were present at the last minute of the mother's life and that they were able to say good-bye to her, even

though they knew such a good-bye would be different than good-byes they usually said to each other. Everybody in the circle almost broke into tears. On these occasions, everybody in the circle feels connected emotionally to everyone else because everybody's reaction to the stories are almost the same. Without the JAS space and values, I don't think Kate or Raymond would have been able to share their stories. This is how community is built—when people of diverse backgrounds become witnesses to each other's lives in such a space.

Kari: Do you see Somali and U.S.-born people learning the ideas and practices that will help them participate actively in a democratic society?

Ahmed: Here in the United States, the word *democracy* is used in public conversation on a daily basis, yet people often do not talk about its underlying meanings. They often underestimate the many democratic opportunities they have in this country, such as free elections, individual freedoms, and voting rights. All immigrants and college students at JAS have the opportunity to learn and teach what it means to be a citizen living in a democratic country. At JAS, some college students who grew up in the United States seem to take democracy for granted. In contrast, many JAS immigrants who come from countries that don't have a democratic-based system see basic elements of democracy in America more easily than the native participants do.

Some college students take for granted the right to criticize the U.S. government for not improving the existing democratic system. Many immigrants appreciate the freedom to engage in such criticism of democracy because they come from countries where they couldn't criticize or question their governments. Some students have a narrow view of the world and seem to think only within the context of the United States. Regarding politics, they seem to me to be internally focused; they don't know a lot about international politics. In Somalia, conversation about world affairs is always in the air. People are aware of what is going on in many parts of the world.

At JAS, we discuss these political and ideological issues as a group despite our differences. When we talked about the war in Iraq, for instance, some Somalis felt America attacked Iraq because of the oil. Some within the American group held the same view; others held a different view. We all had the opportunity to exercise our freedom of speech. We all used the democratic space to practice freedom of expression right there in the circle.

The different ways in which people in a democracy think is changing among those of us who come to JAS. It's changing with me and I see it changing with others too. I have seen U.S.-born citizens think differently about democracy because of their interaction with people of Somalia. When immigrants talk about the civil war in Somalia and the 21 years of military rule and how oppressive it was, the native students first become aware of the history and might appreciate their system of government more. This gives native students an opportunity to explain and reflect on American democracy. In contrast, Somali participants learn about the American democracy and its election processes. This exchange of history and governmental information between the two groups helps people recognize that there are viable worldviews different than their own. They recognize that despite the differences, communities can form.

Kari: Do you think the work we do to prepare for the citizenship test contributes to learning about democracy?

Ahmed: If immigrants learn the answers only for the test, JAS is not doing its job. Teaching U.S. history to immigrants who don't speak the language doesn't ensure they learn the *meanings* of citizenship and democracy. More time should be spent on learning what these concepts mean to us. Otherwise, they are just symbolic notions that we safeguard. We need to emphasize that citizenship is more than paying taxes and voting. JAS is a place where immigrants can prepare themselves to take the citizenship test *and* learn to express their views in public—to see how other people express their opinions. In a democracy, people have to listen and learn to compromise. We want immigrants to leave JAS with a rich understanding of what citizenship and democracy mean. Learning how to engage in a democratic dialogue is important because you never know— some of us might go back to Somalia one day and find these concepts useful.

Kari: *At JAS, we insist that everyone teaches and everyone learns. Do you think this contributes to building a democratic culture?*

Ahmed: When I sit back and watch the East African Circle, I see the formation of a community. I see people who are trying to connect with each other. They use whatever skills work for them to communicate with one another. Since there is no teacher who instructs them, everyone is a teacher and everyone is a learner. People interact and exchange their personal stories in a lively way. We become a community of people who come together to learn with each other.

This type of gathering is totally different than that of students gathering in a class at the University of Minnesota and listening to a professor/teacher. Students in a class don't interact with each other but simply sit upright and recite back what they have learned. Learning at JAS is reciprocal. We build a community among a group of individuals different in so many ways.

Kari: *You've been describing a set of practices and values we aspire to at JAS. What kind of possibility do you see coming from this experience?*

Ahmed: I see hope. I see a vision for one world, not two, as

we try to honor each other in our similarities and differences. People can build relationships across these differences. This gives me hope. I am still perplexed about what is happening in Somalia, which has had no government for 15 years. The main problem among warlords has been conflict over who would be the president. They have

redrawn an ancient tradition of clan policy. Why do we have to judge people in terms of clans?

At JAS, I have felt that human beings can have peace in this world despite differences in race, ethnicity, culture, religion, and traditions. To be honest, I did not learn this in my country. Every night when I go to bed, I lie awake thinking about the situation in Somalia. I worry that I will never see my home country again. Like other Somalis, however, I keep my fingers crossed that one day there might be a legitimate government in our country based on democracy with freedom of association, speech, press, and the right to vote. I've learned at JAS. . . that no matter the differences, people can come together and build a peaceful environment if they want to. My major [at the University of Minnesota] is government and peace studies. I realized the importance of peace after the civil war in my country. I had not thought about it before then. I always leave JAS with the hope that this is possible.

BRIDGING THE AMERICAS

by Eduardo Jurado

The immigrants who meet at the Jane Addams School for Democracy see that we are part of a long history. The first settlers in this land were Native Americans. Later, people arrived from Spain and Northern Europe. Now, in the twenty-first century, immigrants come from Asia, Africa, and South America. When we arrive, many of us don't know how to speak English or how to find work. Making the transition to a new country is very difficult. But after a while you learn you can do things on your own—go to school, find a job, make a new life. Then you fly with your own wings.

I quickly learned that JAS is a bridge between people who are new to the United States and the people who have always lived here. New immigrants come to JAS to improve their English for school and work, but they can also learn about the culture and lifestyle in the United States. Immigrants have a hunger to learn these things. We also encounter people who are open to learning about us and interested in understanding our cultures. When people ask me about my home, I tell them "I am an American too, from South America." People who are Cubans, Mexicans, Guatemalans, Argentinians, or Peruvians understand we are part of the Americas, even though some born in the United States may be surprised to hear us call ourselves Americans.

At JAS, people from all over the world tell about the cultures of their countries and regions. It would not be easy for me to travel to places like Thailand, Vietnam, East Africa, Japan, or Western Europe. When I hear people talk about these cultures and exchange ideas about music, dance, and traditional clothing, I see similarities as well as differences. When I lived in Peru, I had never heard of the Hmong people; here in Minnesota I've learned about their culture. I learned, for example, that Hmong traditional clothing uses colors that are quite similar to colors in the clothing worn in the Andes Mountains in Peru. The dress is different, but the colors are the same. There are some words in Chinese that are related to the Incan culture. I can see similarities in their facial characteristics with Andes people. How did this happen when the two cultures are so far away from each other? For me, it's quite amazing to think about.

JAS is a school for everyday life that provides the kind of education that you don't get from the newspaper. Much of our work together helps people—newcomers and native born—learn what living in a democracy means. We hold mock elections to practice the mechanics of voting. We organize candidate forums. We build skills when we discuss topics together. People bring their own viewpoints—their agreements and disagreements—and still talk with each other in a respectful way. This is what democracy is about—the opportunity to express ideas, develop positions, and figure out what to do together.

We often talk about exercising our right to freedom of speech, although in the beginning, it was hard for me to express myself. I come from a culture where it can be dangerous to talk about government. I also lived for years in Argentina, where people were also very careful about whom they talked to in public. I had great respect for democracy in

Eduardo Jurado

thoughts, but I also knew there could be problems if I spoke about it openly. Many who did were accused of being Communists or terrorists. There is no freedom of expression back home. When I told my parents about the people at JAS and the work we do, my mother warned, "There may be security agents who could get you in trouble." She grew up—with fear. At JAS, I eventually learned to speak openly without fear. We may not agree with another person, but we listen to each other respectfully. Although I was in the United States on a student visa at that time, I went to the legislature to talk with representatives and senators. In my country, politicians would not listen to noncitizens. But here, everyone has the opportunity to talk with elected officials. It gives a wonderful taste of democracy. This is my experience of freedom.

I think it is important to promote democracy in a country like the United States where people don't need to vote. In Peru, people pay a fine for not voting and cannot hold a government job until the fine is paid. In the United States, people are granted this wonderful democracy, and many don't bother to vote until problems come up. So I feel promoting democracy for those who are indifferent is crucial, especially at this time when citizens need to assume responsibility and power. Right now I am not allowed to vote, but I'm happy to help other people prepare for voting through education. I've also found other ways to participate in this democracy.

I worked with the Minnesota Immigrant Workers Freedom Ride to push for reform of immigration policy. It was a national event modeled after the freedom rides during the civil rights movement. Participating with the Freedom Riders gave me the exciting opportunity to explain to people I met along the way about the rights that everyone has in this country. The U.S. Constitution applies to everyone living in the country—citizen or not. So we explained that many people were suffering from persecution because they were not U.S. citizens. In southern Minnesota, for example, we found a family who had citizenship papers, but because they were Mexican and didn't speak English well, they felt isolated. They were abused at their jobs. We were together, marching with them on the streets. We were not there to make trouble but to protect our rights. JAS joined with me in this work.

At JAS, we work to change the rules. "No" is not the solution for the people here. We get things done because there is communication and cooperation. Over the years, we've tackled problems large and small. I remember when the Hmong people could not get their families out of Laos. We appealed to elected authorities to do something about it. We worked on the Dream Act, which would help immigrants without proper papers go to college paying in-state tuition. We talked with legislators and wrote many letters. In the end, the bill did not pass, but it was close. We'll try again. Change takes time.

JAS shows how new Americans of many backgrounds can work together and communicate across cultures. It is also a window for people who are not immigrants. People who have traveled overseas and know what it feels like to be the stranger in a country that is not their home tend to treat foreigners here with respect. People who have not had these experiences—who have never traveled to the Third World or who have traveled only in the United States, Canada, or Europe—can learn that respect at JAS. If they are patient enough to listen to us newcomers, they begin to see that we all share many similarities—we all have families; we go to school; we raise children.

People also begin to understand the real differences. When you live in a country that has plenty of technology and a good economy, it's important to learn that resources are different in other countries and that people have to achieve their goals differently. As we listen to each other's life stories, we can begin to understand how people have had to adapt in the world. We become sympathetic to each other's reality. Learning from each other firsthand helps us understand this is *one* planet, *one* world. As we support each other, we take care of the whole planet.

SHAPING CONNECTIONS WITH HIGHER EDUCATION

by Nan Kari

The Jane Addams School for Democracy resides in the between—*a metaphoric location that bridges the neighborhood with the academy. This intercultural space found at the intersection of colleges and neighborhoods creates rich opportunities to deepen our collective understanding of how diverse people work together for common purpose.* It also suggests a slightly different framework than that implied in more traditional college-community partnerships.

Over the past ten years, partly in response to growing public skepticism about the enormous investment in post-secondary education, institutions of higher education have taken seriously broad questions of public accountability and effectiveness, especially in educating democratic citizens for a global age. Working *in* public and *with* the public is at the heart of these discussions. National education associations, foundations, and universities and colleges have launched a myriad of symposia, research efforts, high-level commissioned reports, and on-the-ground projects. In 1999, for instance, more than 300 college presidents and deans signed the *Presidents' Declaration on the Civic Responsibility of Higher Education*, a National Campus Compact document that called for a recommitment of higher education institutions to their civic missions.

> How can we realize this vision of institutional public engagement? . . . It will require our hard work, as a whole, and within each of our institutions. We will know we are successful by the robust debate on our campuses and by the civic behaviors of our students. We will know it by the civic engagement of our faculty. We will know it when our community partnerships improve the quality of community life and the quality of education we provide.[1]

In 2000, the Kellogg Commission on the Future of State and Land-Grant Universities issued a letter to the public called *Renewing the Covenant*. This report, the culmination of an extensive national study about how to renew land-grant missions, was written with a sense of urgency that our nation's success in a changing world depends on the recommitment of these institutions to public engagement.

At the University of Minnesota, President Robert Bruininks instituted a permanent Council on Public Engagement (COPE), a high-level university committee charged with ensuring the integration of civic learning and public engagement throughout the institution—reflected in classrooms, faculty and staff work, and in partnerships with Minnesotans outside the university. COPE's purpose is to transform the institution's culture so that it becomes a publicly engaged university. In a 2004 study, COPE named the university's partnership with JAS as one of several effective models for civic learning. In 2005, Macalester College and JAS were identified as one of eight exemplary campus-community partnerships by the National Campus Compact research effort commissioned by the Knight Foundation. In their

site visit, Edward Zlotkowski and Jennifer Meeropol (National Campus Compact) described the learning at JAS as central to the academic undertaking, rather than a marginal activity, with important implications for students' civic learning and also for research epistemology and methods.

These public initiatives, in their many iterations, form an important backdrop to the practical on-the-ground work of forging effective partnerships between neighborhoods and colleges. The national conversation draws attention to the largest questions of improving our collective lives as we educate our children and ourselves to participate fully in a democratic society. We at JAS have jumped into the conversation with both feet, believing that our experience in working "in the intersection" can both contribute to, and benefit from, this important public work.

How people conceptualize college-community partnerships matters. The framework defines roles and expectations; it carries assumptions about power and knowledge; and it influences the nature of the relationships formed among people and between

organizations and higher education, thus shaping the processes and outcomes of the shared work. Forming and sustaining partnerships between neighborhoods and institutions of higher education are complex, multilayered, political endeavors. Too often the language used to describe it oversimplifies the process.

A few years ago, a talented community organizer, new to the academy, convened a small invited group of people from across the country to "push the edges," as she said, on the formulation of college-community partnerships. Could an organizing lens expand how we conceptualize relationships? A mixed group of people from inside and outside the academy, who had given thought to the challenges and practices of such affiliations, participated in the dialogue. Three of us from JAS attended. I went with the expectation that the public conversation would call us at JAS to articulate more clearly the intended purposes of our higher education affiliations and help us better define the model we saw emerging.

As we flew out on the plane, we discussed how we would introduce our partnership. Want-

Macalester College

The University of Minnesota

The College of
St. Catherine

ing to avoid the constraints of the typical partnership categories—student, faculty, community organization staff, or neighborhood resident—we decided to

introduce ourselves in terms of the constituencies we bring to the work. See Moua, holds cultural knowledge and relationships within the Hmong community;

she has strong relationships with neighborhood children and their parents as well as with college students she helps recruit and mentor. Her office is at the university. Nan Skelton brokers relationships with the St. Paul school district and school board; she maintains contact with long-time community leaders, relationships established from her earlier days working as a community organizer and later, as assistant commissioner for education. She now codirects the Center for Democracy and Citizenship. Her office is at the university, but she also identifies strongly with the neighborhood. And I, having been a faculty member at the College of St. Catherine for more than 20 years, also plant my feet firmly on both sides of the border, identifying strongly with academic cultures, college students, and faculty, while feeling a strong pull to relationships with leaders in ethnic communities and others on the West Side involved in larger questions of neighborhood revitalization. The fluidity of roles and the ability to navigate metaphorical borders shape the partnerships JAS forms and encourages those involved to think from multiple points of view—a skill set that is key to democratic education.

Imagine our frustration then, when the symposium convener tried earnestly to help the JAS team back into the boxes. Probably she wanted to initiate the discussion by offering a familiar map. But the map narrowed our roles and denied the idea that

people have civic identities as well as those of faculty, students, and community members. This tension brought into relief the emergent patterns we have begun to recognize through our experience at JAS.

Across the country there are many fine examples of sustained college-community partnerships that have produced remarkable public outcomes. Partnerships form for a variety of purposes and use different frameworks. Yet the universal categories used to describe the partners and the players build artificial boundaries

that can limit how people experience power, reciprocity, and cocreation. Perhaps more important, they impede the ability to cross borders and to exercise legitimate authority. When, for instance, we talk about faculty and community members, does this imply that faculty must remain on the outside, apart from the community? If we talk about teaching and learning, does it follow that the college-affiliated people are the teachers and the community members the learners? Does the "doing" happen in the real world of neighbor-

JAS college students dressed in traditional Hmong garments at the annual Freedom Festival

hoods and the "meaning making" inside the academy? And are there public purposes for college-community partnerships that go beyond contributing knowledge and people to address unmet needs in the community? We would argue that the dominant framework and the "shorthand" language imply a hierarchy that privileges theoretical knowledge and professional credentials, assigning academics and other professionals to the top rungs and community members and students to the bottom.

The symposium did allow space to challenge partnership categories, but mostly the group did not have the language or perhaps enough reflected experience to articulate an alternative framework. The concluding session was led by a seasoned academic—a longstanding leader in the service-learning movement—who focused his discussion questions around the tired old problems of how to get faculty members to value community-based learning; how to lead classroom reflection sessions that help students stitch together theory with their real-world observations; and how to rework the promotion and tenure

system to reward action research and community involvement, often referred to as faculty service. While these are all viable questions, this framework puts the conversation squarely inside the academy, which then limits who participates in creating a different vision about what is possible.

Emerging Patterns and Themes

The JAS tie to higher education has never been in question. We founded JAS with the intent of providing a radically different kind of education for students. The collective experiences of the founders interacting with students in the classroom and in a variety of venues over the years had taught us that college students often experience a sense of disconnection from real life, which the academic community does not, and perhaps cannot on its own, adequately address. The focus on abstract theoretical knowledge creates an intellectual culture somewhat distanced from knowledge gained from experience. Young men and women frequently tell us how their age-segregated college experience distances them from children and

elders and sometimes from their cultures of origin. JAS, inspired by the belief that place—its history, geography, accomplishments, problems, and especially its people—the textured stuff of neighborhoods, creates an essential context for learning. Over time and through much dialogue, we have come to better understand two core, interdependent ideas: community and diversity.

Community

Themes of community run throughout these essays as an essential backdrop for learning and meaning making from reflected experience. *Community*, however, is a nebulous term, a word applied liberally, often with political overtones in current public conversation. Community can refer to geographic place, affinity groups of gender, faith, political persuasion, and ethnic groups. For some, community means an intensely personal experience. Others see themselves as part of large communities of loosely formed relationships.

We use the term at JAS in the context of a learning community—a community with webs of relationships, shared work, and patterns of meaning making that promote and support learning for everyone. We hypothesize that diverse, egalitarian relationships are best formed within a community attentive both to personal relationships and to shared public purpose.

Although ideas about community building have animated our work from the beginning, I resisted the use of community language for a long time, thinking that the word *community* conjured an idealized, almost nostalgic state, which covered the "real" politics with diversity and power differences. I've come to think differently. The weakening of neighborhoods, paired with the growing sense of isolation and divisions among people, result from a frayed web of relationships and a diminishing sense of connection to others outside the circle of family and friends. This loss contributes to the general sense that people are not rooted in real communities of place anymore—a serious threat currently undermining our democratic society. Social critics and other observers point to multiple, complex factors to account for the weakening of neighborhoods and communal ties, among them: high mobility and urban design

oriented toward the automobile; in some places, a school choice option that sends children to public schools distant from their neighborhoods; and growing economic stress, which often results in more time spent at work, away from home.

The loss of connectedness among people is exacerbated by the scarcity of places where people can establish cross-cultural relationships in public settings. In the West Side neighborhood, people on the street speak proudly of its cultural diversity and its long immigrant history. They readily point to the many examples of ethnic public murals adorning businesses and public parks. But they also say with some regret, that there are few places where people of diverse ethnicities can interact meaningfully with each other. Often these relationships, when they happen, form around tutoring or other one-way, charity-based exchanges. The barriers to egalitarian relationships are real: differences in languages, customs, world views, education, and economic status. All help erect walls that impede relationships and understanding across cultures.

JAS creates an important pub-

lic space and communal context within which to build relationships across age, culture, and language groups, and it provides a vehicle for faculty and students to establish authentic relationships with a mixed group of people while they explore a variety of intellectual and practical questions about themselves and larger public issues.

JAS participants describe their communal experience in a variety of ways. Kari Denissen, a 2000 graduate of the university and later a neighborhood resident and West Side "community connector" for the Neighborhood Learning Community,[2] recalls:

> [JAS] attracted me because you aren't just a volunteer, it's about the relationships. Once you form authentic relationships and become part of a community, you also have a sense of obligation to the community and it is harder to leave. In 1999, I wasn't living on a campus anymore, and I didn't feel like I had a community. It's hard to find community in college, because the places where college students live tend to be neighborhoods where there's such high turnover that it's hard to be part of community, at least in a neighborhood sense. When

University of Minnesota professor Harry Boyte (right) talks with Miami University professor Nick Longo and Macalester College student Stephanie Raill about academic/community connections.

you move a lot, you need to find a place more stable that you can call your community. JAS became that for me. When you claim a group in this way, you don't want to leave. It's not like you finish the internship project and say, "I'll see you later." I felt an obligation and I got a lot out of it too . . . mentorship and perspective. I also felt critical about some things, and I did not want to be the kind of person who wouldn't stay to work things through. I wanted to help change it, grow with it, and learn in the process.[3]

Other students seek community at JAS in part to reconnect with elders and children of similar cultural backgrounds. For many second-generation immigrants, the college experience can engender a sense of alienation from the lived experiences of their families and thus people feel distanced from cultural identities when they become part of an academic culture. Participating in a community that recognizes cultural knowledge invites a reconnection with cultural groups of origin and reaffirms important aspects of individual identity. Interacting with adults of their parents' and grandparents' ages fills a void for young people who learn again to appreciate the contributions of elders. Pakou Hang explains:

> In the Hmong community we believe that the children are the future of the community. But at the same time, as a young person, you have to learn you are standing on the shoulders of your elders. JAS offers the space for these conversations. I think that's very powerful.[4]

Often, on first impulse, students describe the JAS community in terms of cross-cultural friendships. Students come alive with stories of new friendships, invitations to participate in others' cultural traditions, and sometimes to make transnational connections with family members. Indeed, these powerful, and often, sustained friendships form the glue that keeps people involved over many years, well beyond college graduation. But the public dimension of community can be equally powerful. Though people in the Hmong Circle may not know members of the Spanish-Speaking or the East African circles well, it matters that there is a larger "we." The broad vision to engage people as active agents in a shared public life cannot be achieved through a focus on individual relationships alone, regardless of the depth of personal reward or transformative power. It is this larger public community that forms an important context for civic learning for students, faculty, and immigrant families.

Diversity

To speak of the college-community partnership, as a relationship between the college and the neighborhood or a community organization oversimplifies a complicated set of relationships, diverse interests, and sometimes stunning cultural differences among people engaged in the experience, thus hiding tensions that arise from conflicting assumptions or misunderstanding. Inside these frustrations and conflicts, however, reside powerful learning opportunities.

College students sometimes experience a "cultural clash" when they first come to JAS. Reflective essays written at the conclusion of the experience for their course work can reveal dramatically different interpretations of what appears to be, on the surface, a common experience. This is when the partnership framework makes a difference.

Students, and sometimes faculty, frequently think of work in community organizations or neighborhoods as an opportunity to "give back" in acknowledgment of privilege, or as a venue to gain firsthand knowledge about societal problems. Too often, contribution is the focus from the classroom and foremost on students' minds. On the other side, community organizations, struggling with scarce resources and a growing demand for services, often welcome volunteer help to fill the gap. Indeed, neighborhoods undertaking significant redevelopment projects or schools seeking to improve children's reading embrace these examples of college-community partnerships.

But the focus of JAS partnerships differs. If our primary task is to build a vibrant and diverse community of learners, then to invite students, faculty or, for that matter, partnering institutions, to primarily "help" immigrants become citizens is a philosophic mismatch. This is not to say that students and faculty don't make significant contributions as learning partners with non-native English speakers. But a helping concept carries assumptions about roles and power—

often unexamined—that counter the egalitarian democratic environment we aim to create and sustain. Because students tend to be familiar with the service framework and the primacy of academic knowledge, tension arises when they encounter the JAS culture, in which we ask newcomers simply to find membership in a diverse community.

In the early years, we struggled to find ways to help newcomers negotiate the dissonance many experience as they try to find their way in unfamiliar territory, where norms and expectations are slightly different than anticipated and roles are not immediately clear. At first we were inclined to preempt student discomfort by easing them into a different set of expectations. We tried to "fix" their uneasiness with explanations and solutions, only to realize that experiencing cultural differences and finding one's way through the discomfort into community membership is likely one of the key learning experiences at JAS.

Storytelling is a useful tool in bridging cultures. Academic environments teach processes like literature reviews, research, writing, and presentation as

paths toward knowing. In addition to these processes, JAS emphasizes the importance of lived experience discovered through storytelling and dialogue as viable routes to new knowledge. Students of European descent sometimes tell us they are not aware of their own cultures and thus have difficulty crafting personal narratives for public sharing. When people become distanced from their cultural stories or unable to reflect on the meanings of their lived experiences, it becomes more difficult to enter another's reality.

Sharing personal and collective narratives helps facilitate skills needed to understand self and others and to make meaningful connections across cultures. Without these skills, people are often left to objectify others.

In Minnesota, a 2005 study commissioned by former vice president Walter Mondale examined the state of Minnesota's communities, with startling results.[5] Even though immigration is up only 5 percent compared with a high mark of 30 percent in the 1930s, a disturbing number of Minnesotans now point to the

College students Joel Ulrich and Koshin Ahmed

JAS college students: (back row standing from left) Yang Vue, Ted Roethke, Moua Xiong, Luke Stevens, Kong Vang, and Joel Ulrich; (front row from left) Mee Cheng, Koshin Ahmed, Derek Johnson

influx of new immigrants and refugees as the primary cause of the stresses and strains on the state's budget and the perceived decline of community. These attitudes were particularly true of residents in ex-urban areas, a trend seen across the United States.

This alarming tendency to lay the state's problems at the feet of new immigrants gives a sense of urgency to the creation of public space and opportunity for cross-cultural teaching and learning, a shared task for partners within and outside higher education. Authorship of a shared public narrative is part of cocreating a public life. Crafting a collective narrative has relevance both to JAS and its academic partners. It contributes to the larger story we tell about who we are and what we can be together.

Creating Partnerships

Relationships between JAS and institutions of higher education develop over time and with different levels of intensity. They rarely begin in administrators' offices. Typically colleges and community organizations form partnerships with a specific task in mind, often to seek funds—to tutor children in reading; to bring community youth on campus; to establish community clinics and the like. Impressive publications showcase the partnership and its outcomes. Though productive, these partnerships are often one-dimensional, particularly when the responsibility for building and sustaining the relationship falls to a few designated people—someone on campus and a "partner" in a community nonprofit. In contrast, JAS builds relationships with colleges "brick by brick" in multidimensional ways and with many people involved: through shared research, curriculum development, faculty development, student work-study, and internships. In its largest framing we describe the JAS-college affiliation in terms of shared public work to build civic skills so that diverse people can cocreate a better common life.

Although people usually don't initiate partnerships based on an abstract idea, the power of public work as an animating concept becomes evident when people see concrete products resulting from their shared effort. When Macalester College and JAS, for instance, convened a symposium for discussion of reconceptualizing citizenship at the college, new citizens gave short public

reflections and helped facilitate round-table discussions with students. Through this work a more textured, multidimensional sense of partnership began to emerge. In another example, the JAS partnership with the College of St. Catherine was strengthened when Hmong women, experienced with textiles, co-taught a seminar with a professor teaching a course on sociocultural components of clothing. Classes were convened both on campus and at JAS. In both instances, the public work gave visibility to a beginning partnership, which opened opportunities to explore ideas and initiate new endeavors in multiple areas.

We have learned that robust partnerships in which many people claim ownership must be stitched into the structures and practices of both JAS and the academic institution. When many people are connected in multiple ways and when they make their work visible, the collective relationships reach a tipping point, and an authentic college-community partnership forms.

At any given time, JAS might include graduate and undergraduate students from the University of Minnesota, the College of St.

Catherine, Macalester College, the University of St. Thomas, St. Olaf College, Metro State University, Augsburg College, Century College, and students affiliated with the Higher Education Consortium for Urban Affairs (HECUA). To say that JAS has a partnership with each of these institutions would be inaccurate. Yet it is student involvement that often provides the opening for a working relationship with an institution.

College and university students come to JAS in many ways: as service learners affiliated with a variety of courses from public policy to textile design to philosophy; they participate as interns able to contribute 10–20 hours per week; others use JAS as their work-study assignment. The latter two ways especially, require an established relationship with career services or service-learning offices on campus, which sometimes becomes a starting point for a more formal institutional relationship. In other instances, students come with their instructor, who includes the time spent at JAS as part of the class requirement. The advantage to this arrangement is that the professor shares the experience with her students and can better facilitate integration of experiential learning with course theory. On the other hand, the required participation takes away student choice, which sometimes leads to resistance and a sense that the experience is an imposed assignment. This runs counter to the JAS philosophy that people are active learners not recipients of someone else's direction.

Generally, the students who come through work-study, internships, and AmeriCorps positions, form the core group of highly engaged people who shape the day-to-day work along with the JAS organizers. Many in this group are bilingual and assume important roles as interpreters. People in this group play an essential bridging role between JAS and their home institutions.

Faculty involvement also provides an entrée to institutional partnership. A growing number of faculty members have integrated the JAS experience with their course work and offer it as one of several semester-long community-learning options. Others who staff service-learning and work-study centers also encourage student involvement on a regular basis. These kinds of

ongoing connections lay the groundwork for deeper institutional relationships.

Conclusion

We regularly convene a lively college-JAS seminar, which includes faculty and staff who have had sustained involvement with JAS in a variety of ways. We gather for dinner and use a learning-circle format to share ideas and delve into questions core to our shared work. Many of these self-named partners have themselves participated as learners at JAS. In our discussions we struggle with issues of college-community partnerships. What is the role of the academy in the community? How do neighborhood experiences contribute to theory building? How can faculty participate in neighborhoods in meaningful and sustained ways? How would people describe the JAS partnership model? we asked one evening. Pondering this, the group created a definition:

> We're a "network of tricksters" —subversive, somewhat wily companions on a journey together—able to support the journey with multiple talents, perspectives, and innate ingenuity. Somewhere along the way we invite our institutions to make the voyage.

Indeed, these are elements essential to the kind of partnerships JAS seeks to build.

---

[1] Thomas Ehrlich and Elizabeth Hollander, *Presidents' Declaration on the Civic Responsibility of Higher Education* (Providence, RI: Campus Compact, 1999), 4.

[2] The Neighborhood Learning Community is a neighborhood-based public work initiative, which JAS helped to launch in 2001, with the broad goal to cocreate a culture of learning in the West Side neighborhood. JAS remains a key partner in the work. The community connector role is a key organizing position responsible for making connections among and between neighborhood residents and staff of local nonprofit organizations.

[3] Kari Denissen, interview conducted by N. Kari for the Partnership Subcommittee of the University of Minnesota's Committee on Public Engagement, February 2004.

[4] Pakou Hang, interview conducted by N. Kari for the Partnership Subcommittee of the University of Minnesota's Committee on Public Engagement, February 2004.

[5] *The Changing Shape of Minnesota: Reinvigorating Community and Government in the New Minnesota.* Report. Prepared for the Minnesota Community Project by Stan Greenberg, Anna Greenberg, and Julie Hootkin, December 14, 2004. <http://www.greenbergresearch.com

AFTERWORD

by David Mathews

Recently, the Kettering Foundation was visited by a group of citizens, largely from Kentucky, who are trying to improve the public schools, specifically those in small, rural communities. The Kentuckians are a mixed lot: some describe themselves as grandparents, some as principals of alternative schools, some as former academics. They share one uniting conviction: a community is an educational agency itself and capable of reinforcing learning in the schools. The Kentuckians have wonderful stories of what this book calls "public work," which is being used both to build communities and educate young people. The work covers a broad spectrum, including caring for retired racehorses, reintroducing a blight-resistant variety of chestnut trees, and recovering local history by collecting old photographs. The significance of these projects isn't in their subjects (horses, chestnut trees, old photographs); it is in the work that citizens do to organize the projects and use them in teaching children.

The political genius of the Kentuckians is in connecting these projects to form a network throughout the state, a network that could be a force in restoring public ownership of public education. Making connections is a different strategy from trying to get individual projects up to scale. The Kentuckians want farmers to plant corn in support of the veterinarians who care for the horses. They hope that some chemist might join them to demonstrate how methane could be generated from the manure. This network-building strategy illustrates a very important insight. Many community-based learning projects have developed in isolation and then faded away. The Kentuckians know that, in order to survive, the individual projects have to connect to one another—and to something larger.

I am sending our friends in Kentucky this book because it is about connecting to something larger. It locates community-based projects in education in the continuing struggle to rule our-selves—our struggle to maintain a democratic way of life. And this book is very specific about the kind of democracy that it advocates; it is a democracy in which citizens are producers of education, not just consumers of school services.

Voices of Hope: The Story of the Jane Addams School for Democracy *couldn't be timelier. It comes at a point when Americans are trying to reclaim ownership of the education of children through community projects like those in Kentucky. It also comes at a time when schools are trying to reengage their communities and communi-ties are trying to reengage their citizens. As has been observed, we spent most of the twentieth century learning how to build large institutions and forgetting how to build communities—only to arrive at the eve of the twenty-first century with problems that couldn't be solved without whole villages being involved. The University of Minnesota, where Nan Skelton is located, must*

have come to a similar conclusion because the institution takes its civic engagement seriously. (In fact, the Jane Addams School experiment is giving a distinctive meaning to university engage-ment because it is self-conscious about the kind of democracy it is promoting.)

Most important of all, this story is being told at a time when the meaning of democracy is being debated around the world. The established institutional and procedural concepts of democracy (in which citizens are less directly involved as voters or clients) are being challenged by notions of self-rule that envision citizens as active sovereigns. These chal-lenges are probably a reaction to measures that have sidelined citizens or reduced them to politi-cal consumers, a displacement carefully documented by Matthew Crenson and Benjamin Ginsberg in Downsizing Democracy.[1]

The Minnesota project is clearly linked to something larger. Because the founders of the Jane Addams School for Democracy have organized their efforts

around well-defined concepts of democracy and education, they have something to offer those who are undertaking similar experi-ments. And the story of the Jane Addams School also has some-thing to say to foundations and other institutions that would like to assist such experiments.

The founders did not do what is normally done, which is to imitate best practices, lay out a precise plan of action, and for-mulate goals that would yield measurable evidence of impact. Knowing that most grantmakers would impose those conditions and that they would not be con-ducive to experimentation, they decided not to rely on foundation funding. Grantmakers who hope to promote innovations should take note. They have to attract, not drive away, inventive civic entrepreneurs. The founders of JAS could not tell foundations what they were going to discover because they had to "make the road by walking." That is, they could not follow a predetermined plan to a predetermined destina-tion. They followed a conceptual map, which took them into unexplored territory.

This conceptual clarity has led the Jane Addams School to some powerful insights. For instance, citizens can be teachers. *Years before JAS was founded, the Hubert H. Humphrey Institute of Public Affairs at the University of Minnesota ran an experiment with citizens who might seem the least likely to be teachers—people with limited formal education living in poor neighborhoods. Nonetheless, the research showed that these citizens had a variety of valuable experiences and skills to share with youngsters. Other studies have found similar evidence. One that was done for the Kettering Foundation with members of inner-city churches was based on a series of questions: What do you know how to do well? Where did you learn it? What helped you learn it? Have you ever taught anyone anything? What do you think made your teaching effective?[2] The church members' first reaction was, "I never taught anybody anything," perhaps because they associated*

teaching with classrooms. When pressed, however, most everyone could recall several ways in which they had, in fact, educated young people. They had taught basic reading and mathematics as well as skills like cooking, sewing, and taking care of equipment. Their "lessons" included the virtues of patience, persistence, and sacrifice.

Communities aren't assumed to have that substantive academic information—only practical tips on how to get along in the world. That assumption just isn't valid, as the JAS project demonstrates. Community institutions can't replace the schools, yet many of them teach the same subjects taught in classrooms. Two obvious examples: natural history museums offer courses in ecology, and art museums teach art history.

In fact, the potential for school-community collaboration in academic fields is enormous. A Kettering study of seven cities across the country found a broad spectrum of local organizations teaching subjects that might supplement school curricula. The list of organizations included eight

science museums, four history museums, two art museums, seven theaters, one choir, one orchestra, and four libraries. Thirteen other institutions— for example, the Latin American Family Day Center in Charlotte, North Carolina; the YMCA in Willimantic, Connecticut; the North Carolina Zoological Park in Asheboro, North Carolina; and the Trailside Nature Center in Cincinnati, Ohio—also reported offering substantive classes. In just 7 cities, more than 40 teaching organizations were identified with courses ranging from the Ice Age to Egyptian Textiles to the Planetary System.[3]

Courses taught outside the classroom have characteristics that make them ideal for complementing academic instruction. Lauren Resnick's research has shown that schools focus primarily on individual learners, while other community institutions teach youngsters to learn together as part of working together. Her studies also found that schools tend to encourage symbolic and abstract thinking, while instruction outside the school is more likely to be concrete and practical.⁴

Inventories like the one done at Kettering suggest that America could increase its capacity to educate many times over if it harnessed all the educational resources in its communities. The presence of so many educating institutions raises an interesting question: why do boards of education only appoint superintendents of schools? Wouldn't a true board of education be made up of representatives of all of a community's educating institutions? The point here is that citizens have any number of ways to be the authors of the education they would like young people to have.

The learning resources that are created through the collective efforts of citizens are doubly important because the work involved also builds the public— the kind of public that schools and communities need. I don't mean to slight the valuable partnerships schools have formed with businesses and other institutions, but they can't substitute for the

partnerships with a citizenry-at-work.

Clearly, this book isn't about education; it is about democracy and the role of democratic citizens in education. As I said earlier, the story that the authors tell is especially timely because of the debate over what democracy should mean. There are a great many kinds of democracy being promoted these days. The terminology being used is similar, but the role assigned to citizens is key to determining exactly what kind of self-government is envisioned. The Jane Addams School is very explicit about the role it sees for citizens:

> *Put most simply, public work is . . . the visible, sustained efforts of a diverse mix of people that produce goods—material or cultural— of lasting civic value. Citizens are thus cocreators and producers, not only bearers of rights and responsible members of communities.*

In other words, citizens are supposed to make things, and some of the things they make are essential to the education of children.

At Kettering, we have taken this definition of public work and tried to identify the various tasks that are involved when people join forces to make things. The way citizens go about public work is different from the way work is done in professional and bureaucratic settings. If unaware of these differences, citizens as well as professional educators miss opportunities to reinforce one another. They clash instead.

All work is done through carrying out a series of discrete tasks. Take painting a house, for instance. That involves selecting a color, scraping away old paint, priming the surface, and so on. Public work is no different. First of all, people have to identify or name the problems that need attention. Then they have to lay out possible options for solving the problems, which creates the frameworks that will be used in making decisions. And, if they are going to act together, they need to decide together on what should be done. Later, after deciding, citizens have to commit their time and resources, act, and then learn from what happened so they will be better prepared for future problems. There isn't anything extraordinary about these tasks, and there are not special techniques for doing them, although the way citizens go about them is distinctive.

Kettering began its analysis of the components of public work by focusing on how citizens make sound decisions about what work needs to be done and who is to do it. We found answers in the ancient practice of deliberation. Deliberation is both a form of political discourse and a form of politics. Its purpose is to move people from hasty decisions to more reflective and shared judgments about what they should do. Deliberation requires putting all the options for addressing a problem on the table, not just the usual two political positions, and then weighing each option fairly. That is difficult to do, and so deliberation has rightly been called "choice work."

Initially, Kettering concentrated on deliberation as a "different way to talk" and if it hadn't been for people like Nan Kari, Nan Skelton, and their colleague at the Center for Democracy and Citizenship, Harry Boyte, we would have probably stopped there. The challenge of understanding the whole of public work, however, drove us on to look at the role public deliberation can play in helping citizens become producers of publicly useful goods.

Deliberation involves weighing various options for action against what people consider deeply important to their collective well-being. What is deeply important, however, is usually a subject of much disagreement—moral disagreement. Conventional democracy, which is largely institutional and procedural, relies on expert information and majority votes to reach rational decisions. That is all well and good, but moral disagreements are seldom settled by rational arguments. These disagreements can polarize a political system or erupt into violent conflict. Because deliberation takes into consideration what is valuable to people as well as the facts provided by experts, it is better suited to dealing with the disagreements that can stop public work from being done. Public deliberation doesn't end disagreements, however; they are inevitable in a democracy. But deliberation changes the nature of what is being disputed. The disputes are less about exclusive interests (what is good for me and those like me) and more about what is best for all of us.

The idea of public work that is being decided on through deliberative means has also helped the Kettering Foundation do research on what have been called "wicked" problems. These problems abound in neighborhoods like the one where the Jane Addams School is located. They are called wicked problems because they are deeply ingrained in the fabric of a community. They grow out of a weakened feeling of community and then further erode the sense of a commonweal to be protected. A problem is wicked when the diagnosis or definition is unclear, the location or cause is uncertain, and any effective action to deal with it requires narrowing the gap between what is and what ought to be—in the face of disagreement about the latter.[5] Systemic poverty is a good example.

Wicked problems are more human than technical, and they don't respond to professional solutions. When communities are confronted with wicked problems, a shared understanding of the approximate nature of what people are confronting is more important than an immediate solution. In fact, dealing effectively with a wicked problem may depend on not reaching a decision about a solution early on. The ability of citizens to exercise sound judgment in the face of uncertainty is more important than the certainty of experts. Civic commitment trumps an administrative plan. Coping with these problems requires sustained acting that doesn't begin at one point and end at another, but continues in a series of richly diverse initiatives.

Deliberative politics intercepts wicked problems at the points where they are most vulnerable.

It emphasizes the importance of naming problems to reflect all of the varied ways people experience them. It promotes sound collective judgment about what should be done but does not require a consensus, only a shared sense of direction. And deliberative politics can launch an array of public projects, which bring to bear a wide range of community resources.

As you can see, the concept of public work has been enormously useful to the Kettering Foundation. It has helped us better understand all that it takes to make democracy work as it should. Because of our experience, we are convinced this book has accounts of ideas in action that can be useful to others. The Jane Addams School story also illustrates the power of experimentation, which should be commonplace in democratic education. And the greatest insight to take away from this story is how, ultimately, democracy and education are connected. While we are accustomed to hearing the argument that public school-

ing is essential to democracy, this book presents an argument less heard, but equally, if not more important: democracy is essential to education.

---

[1] Matthew A. Crenson and Benjamin Ginsberg, *Downsizing Democracy: How America Sidelined Its Citizens and Privatized Its Public* (Baltimore, MD: Johns Hopkins University Press, 2002).

[2] Project Public Life, *Teaching Politics: A Report from the Third Annual Project Public Life Working Conference* (Minneapolis, MN: Project Public Life, Humphrey Institute of Public Affairs, 1991) and *The Solomon Project Annual Report* (Minneapolis, MN: Project Public Life, Humphrey Institute of Public Affairs, 1992). Also see Doble Research Associates, *Take Charge Workshop Series: Description of Findings from the Field* (Dayton, OH: Report to the Kettering Foundation, 1994).

[3] Kathy Whyde Jesse to David Mathews et al., memorandum, "Newspaper Study," April 18, 1994. Also see Anne T. Henderson and Karen L. Mapp, *A New Wave of Evidence: The Impact of School, Family, and Community Connections on Student Achievement* (Austin, TX: Southwest Educational Development Laboratory, 2002), 8, 68.

[4] Lauren B. Resnick, "Learning In School and Out," *Educational Researcher* 16 (December 1987): 13-20.

[5] The classic reference on wicked problems is Horst W. J. Rittel and Melvin M. Webber, "Dilemmas in a General Theory of Planning," *Policy Sciences* 4 (1973): 155-169.

CONTRIBUTING AUTHORS

Koshin Ahmed

Koshin Ahmed is a student at the University of Minnesota majoring in government and peace studies. He emigrated from Somalia in 2000 after spending ten years in a refugee camp in Kenya. He works at JAS as a facilitator and interpreter in the East African Circle.

Pakou Hang

Born in the Ban Vinai Refugee Camp in Thailand, Pakou Hang immigrated to the United States when she was 15 days old. She graduated from Yale University and is currently in a political science doctoral program at the University of Minnesota.

Derek Johnson

In his work with the Jane Addams School for Democracy over the past five years, Derek Johnson has coordinated the Spanish-Speaking Circle and the East African Circle since its inception. He is a graduate of Brown University. Prior to his work with the Jane Addams School, he was a high-school teacher and worked in a nongovernmental organization in Bogota, Colombia.

Eduardo Jurado

Born in Peru, Eduardo Jurado first came to the United States from South America in 1994 for an international meeting of the Medical Library Association. He returned in 1999 to complete a degree in computer science from St. Paul College in 2003. He has been a participant in the Spanish-Speaking Circle since 2000 and an active leader and promoter of democratic habits at JAS.

Nan Kari

Nan Kari has pursued work for democratic renewal in a variety of contexts since the late 1980s. She was a faculty member at the College of St. Catherine for 20 years and led efforts to revitalize the public culture at the college. She has published many articles and a book on public work and civic renewal. She is a cofounder of the Jane Addams School for Democracy.

D'Ann Urbaniak Lesch

Joining the Jane Addams School in 1997 as an AmeriCorps member with the Center for Democracy and Citizenship, D'Ann Urbaniak Lesch has coordinated the Hmong Circle for almost ten years. Her interest in state and local politics has helped catalyze political work at JAS. She has a master's degree in education.

Gunnar Liden

Gunnar Liden has worked with young people in the West Side neighborhood since 1997. He joined JAS as a college student to help teens organize a homework project. He currently serves as the executive director for the Youth Farm and Market Project, which engages youth in work related to urban agriculture and cultural nutrition. He holds a degree in philosophy.

David Mathews

David Mathews is president of the Charles F. Kettering Foundation. He served as U.S. Secretary of Health, Education, and Welfare in the Ford administration and is a former president of The University of Alabama.

See Moua

As a student at the College of St. Catherine in 1996, See Moua was one of the founders of the Jane Addams School. She began in the role of cultural interpreter in the Hmong Circle and later coordinated the Children's Circle. She is presently pursuing a graduate degree in public health at the University of Minnesota.

Nan Skelton

Nan Skelton codirects the Center for Democracy and Citizenship at the Humphrey Institute of Public Affairs. She has been engaged in many civic projects. Throughout the 1980s, she served as the Assistant Commissioner for Education for the state of Minnesota and continues to lead educational reform efforts. She is a cofounder of the Jane Addams School for Democracy.

See Vang

See Vang emigrated from Thailand to the United States in the 1980s. She gained her U.S. citizenship and is active in her community.

Terri S. Wilson

Terri Wilson came to JAS as a freshman at the University of Minnesota in 1996 and stayed throughout her undergraduate years. She pursued her interest in community- and culturally-based learning through work with the St. Paul Public Schools. She is currently finishing her Ph.D. at Columbia University.

Kathleen Winters

With a strong interest in language learning and the Hmong culture, Kathleen Winters came to JAS through a graduate course at the University of Minnesota. After 34 years teaching high-school French in the public schools, she became a literacy coach at JAS. She continues to pursue her interests in the larger literacy environment.